THE COMPLETE GUIDE TO PROFITABLE REAL ESTATE LISTINGS
Programs of the Pros

The Complete Guide to Profitable Real Estate Listings

Programs of the Pros

F. PETER WIGGINTON

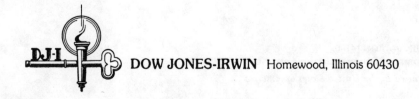
DOW JONES-IRWIN Homewood, Illinois 60430

First Printing, October 1977

ISBN 0-87094-141-0
Library of Congress Catalog Card No. 77-089796
Printed in the United States of America

To Eileen and Lizzie
Patientiam Semper Habentes

Preface

In this book you will discover from the collected accounts of many top listors in the real estate industry how to use their million-dollar listing methods.

No longer—if you ever did have the time—do you have to thumb through the indexes of several books or magazines to dig out information about successful listing. No longer do you have to feel subservient to a fellow salesperson because you have had to ask what he or she does to get those profitable listings. It's all between the covers of this book.

Why should these very successful people reveal their methods of working? There is a curious fact about *big* people—in any walk of life. If their schedules permit, they are willing to explain how they accomplish their goals. They are not miserly with their knowledge. They are not secretive about their methods. They are not envious of another's success.

They know that another person's success, ironically, adds to their own. They know that another person's success eases the tasks necessary to guarantee their own achievements. They know that another person's success helps raise the standards, stature, and professionalism of the entire industry.

Successful people do not wish to see anyone fail. And it is for these reasons the author was able to gather the methods of some *big people* in real estate: the *listing pros* from coast to coast, border to border, throughout the United States.

This book includes their treasury of ideas. Ideas which will enable you to dig deep into your own field of real estate and produce the gems you seek. Armed with the knowledge and practicing the technique of the *listing pros,* you can vault your way over the bars of mediocrity into the arena of the big producers.

September 1977   F. PETER WIGGINTON

Acknowledgments and Sources

This book would not have been possible except for the assistance, cooperation, and contributions of hundreds of professionals from across the United States. From among all these, I wish to especially acknowledge (in alphabetical order) the following who when interviewed graciously shared their expertise:

Loretta Baginski of Laguarta, Gavrel & Kirk, Houston, Texas;

Austin Baker of Clover Realty, Atlanta, Georgia;

Mike Beaton of Schweitzer Real Estate Co., Grosse Pointe Farms, Michigan;

Lucy Ann Bell of Coldwell Banker, Los Angeles (Hancock Park), California;

Dan Bloomquist of Moore Realty, Denver, Colorado;

Lee Burch of Ludlow Realtors®, Inc., Indianapolis, Indiana;

Chuck Cooper of Carolyn Rosen Riteway, Miami, Florida;

Byron Dennis of Bourne-McGehee Realtors®, Jackson, Mississippi;

Don Galemba of Van Schaack & Co., Denver, Colorado;

Mivy Harring of Geer Real Estate Co., Kansas City, Missouri;

Sarah Catherine Holley of Townsend Realty, Charlotte, North Carolina;

Charles Howe of Smith, Bell & Thompson, Burlington, Vermont;

Ruth Hubbard of Donald E. Grempler Realty, Baltimore, Maryland;

Don Jackson of Gifford Realty, Inc., Norfolk, Virginia;

Maurice Johnson of Batt & Miller, Realty One, Buffalo, New York;

Bruce Jorgensen of Bermel Smaby Realty, Minneapolis, Minnesota;

Rosemary Kane of Dayton Cople Realty, Waianae, Hawaii;

Carole Kelby of Thorsen Realty, Chicago, Illinois;

Mike Knapp of Iowa Realty, Des Moines, Iowa;

Jim Kunkel of S. J. Pounder Realty, Portland, Oregon;

Nila Laman of Jack Matthews & Co., Las Vegas, Nevada;

Howard Lubow of Lubow Realty Co., Dayton, Ohio;

Polly Lucas of Donald E. Grempler Realty, Baltimore, Maryland;

Paul Manners of Mile-Hi Realty, Cheyenne, Wyoming;

David McGinnis of Janes & Jacob, Inc., Burlington, Vermont;

Carolyn Rosen Miller of Carolyn Rosen Riteway, Miami, Florida;

Richard Niday of Iowa Realty, Des Moines, Iowa;

Don Nourse of Coldwell Banker, Newport, California;

Ray Novotny of Bermel Smaby Realty, Minneapolis, Minnesota;

G. S. (Skip) Parker of Paul Semonin Co., Louisville, Kentucky;

Veloris Petersen of Bermel Smaby Realty, Minneapolis, Minnesota;

Harry Polay of Gifford Realty, Inc., Norfolk, Virginia;

Eunice Reass of Laguarta, Gavrel & Kirk, Inc., Houston, Texas;

Earl Richardson of Jack Conway & Co., Boston (Cohasset), Massachusetts;

Colleen Rosinbum of Coldwell Banker, Seattle, Washington;

Everett Sanburn of S. J. Pounder Realty, Portland, Oregon;

Gary Shapiro of Price/Shapiro Realtors®, Inc., Scottsdale, Arizona;

Rosamond Shaw of Robert Bruce Realty, Philadelphia, Pennsylvania;

Mike Silverman of Mike Silverman & Associates, Beverly Hills, California;

Jim Spierling of Moore Realty, Denver, Colorado;

Joyce Steffen of Robedeaux, Inc., Milwaukee, Wisconsin;

John Vanneman of Moore Realty, Denver, Colorado;

Eileen Wallen of Hill-Wallen, New Orleans, Louisiana;

Don Weaver of E. J. "Jim" Owen, Realtor®, Columbus, Ohio; David Webster of Gifford Realty, Inc., Norfolk, Virginia.

I am further grateful to the various officers of the Boards of Realtors® in each of the 50 states; to the presidents, owners, and managers of the many cooperating firms; to Bill Moore, Moore Realty, Colorado; and to George Huisken, George Realty, Colorado.

I am indebted to Prentice-Hall, Inc., Englewood, N. J., for permission: to quote from Frederick E. Case, *Real Estate Brokerage,* c. 1965, p. 254, and to quote from Maxwell Maltz, M.D., *Psycho-Cybernetics,* c.1960; to McGraw-Hill Book Co., New York, for permission to quote from Murray Roman, *Telephone Marketing,* c.1976; to the Bobbs-Merrill Co., for permission to quote from F. Peter Wigginton, *Residential Real Estate Practice,* c. 1978; and to Kenneth J. Kerin, for permission to reproduce income figures from *Profile of the Realtor® and Realtor®-Associate* prepared by the Department of Economics and Research of the NATIONAL ASSOCIATION OF REALTORS®.

Acknowledgments would not be complete without expressing appreciation to John M. O'Hara for permission to reproduce materials from R. L. Polk's *City Directory;* V. F. Pyle for permission to reproduce materials from *Cole's Directory;* to Donald H. Johnson for his numerous suggestions, information, and permission to reproduce materials from Real Estate Data, Inc.; and to Joyce A. Little.

F. P. W.

Contents

1

Introduction

"Getting listings is the name of the game," emphasizes Lucy Ann Bell, a 1976 $5 million producer in California, with annual earnings in excess of $100,000.

Ms. Bell has been in the business only five years, and for the past two years she has been number one residential producer nationally for Coldwell Banker. The year before that, she was number one in single-family production. And she has always won her company's listing achievement award.

Here are 11 reasons why Lucy Ann Bell and other top producers spend most of their time developing listings:

1. Listings Offer More Control. Lucy Ann points out that "you control the situation when you have the listing. Even if another broker gets an offer, you control the situation.

"You just can't control a buyer. He may wander into an open house tomorrow and buy it from the listing salesperson. And you're out to lunch.

"But if you have the listing, you get at least half the commission, regardless of who buys the property."

A buyer, then, is very often "flaky." He scurries about on his own in search of property to buy, hopping from one real estate salesperson to another. Regardless of his reasons, the buyer rarely feels any loyalty toward the real estate salesperson. He is seldom willing to be tied to

1

one salesperson. He will switch on a whim, no matter how much time the real estate salesperson has invested in him.

The seller of an Exclusive Listing, on the other hand, has given a contractual promise to be loyal until the sale of the property or termination of the agreement. The listor who obtains an Exclusive Listing works without competition from other real estate salespersons.

2. Listings Fit the Schedule of the Real Estate Salesperson. When working with a buyer, the salesperson must accommodate his or her time to suit the convenience and desires of the client. To help protect his or her growing investment, the salesperson must be prepared to go with the buyer when the buyer wants to go.

When attracted by an ad or a "For Sale" sign, the usual buyer becomes impatient to see a property and rarely wants to wait for a time convenient to the schedule of the salesperson. If one real estate salesperson cannot show the property now, the buyer will try to find another who can.

The listor, however, is not pressured to drop everything and run to the seller. If the listor cannot settle a matter by phone, he or she can, in a professional manner, schedule an appointment with the seller at a time covenient to both of them.

And since the listor can control the times for showings, even with an anxious shopper, the listor can schedule a showing appointment to accommodate his or her own schedule rather than just that of the buyer.

Working by appointment in this way, the listor can make his or her time more productive.

3. Listings Are like Money in the Bank. A listing is almost certain to sell. Even if ony 85 percent to 90 percent of your listings sell, compare this with the 40 percent return a "good" salesperson realizes from his or her investment with buyers, or with the 67 percent return a "top" salesperson achieves when he or she sells two out of every three buyers.

"I generally pursue listings before buyers," says Bruce Jorgensen, sales associate of Bermel Smaby Realty, Minneapolis. "If I can get a listing, I'll go that way. I like to work only with a limited number of prime buyers . . . I spend the rest of my time pursuing listings."

4. Listings Are the Least Expensive Source of Business. Actually, listors need only their feet. They can walk to the site to get a listing. By contrast, the salesperson's chauffering expenses alone amount to a substantial investment.

5. Listings Are the Quickest Method of Obtaining Business. Salespersons normally *wait* for business to come to them. They hope that sometime during floor duty a prospect will walk through the door or that sometime during floor duty a legitimate purchaser will phone and ask a question about real estate.

Listors, on the other hand, go out and *get* what business they want, when they want it, where they want it, and with whom they want it.

6. Listings Are a Source of Other Listings. There are simple, yet effective, methods of ensuring that each listing itself produces several additional listings. These will be described in detail later in this book.

7. Listings Are a Source of Buyers. The quickest and most effective method of obtaining a number of buyers is to have a property listed. Although such buyers frequently discover that your listing is not what they want, if you handle them properly, you can convert them into clients for other listings of yours, or, if you wish, you can turn them over to an associate for a referral fee.

8. Listings Are a Method for Developing a Reputation among Buyers. The successful listor develops a reputation in a given area or community according to the number of times his or her "name riders" and newspaper ads are seen. On the other hand, you never see the name of the person who sells the property.

"I've had a lot of signs up," say Lucy Ann Bell. "I think signs are very helpful. I used to put up as many signs as possible with my name on them so that it became obvious as one drove down the street that I was the leader in the area.

"Lately, I haven't put out many signs, even though I have done a lot of business. But I think my image may be slipping, because another woman in the office has put up signs on everything she has listed, and she is getting a lot more calls than I am. So my signs are back up again. It's an effective way of advertising."

A number of listors recount experiences similar to those of the author of having a buyer at one end of the city phone and ask whether I would find him a house in another part of the city. "Whenever I read the ads in that part of town, the only name I see consistently is yours. You evidently know the market better than anyone else."

After selling one of my listings to that buyer, I colisted his property with an associate working in the buyer's area. That listor, in return, colisted one of his properties with me. In this instance, one phone call soon resulted in the sale of three residences, and there were further results later.

9. Listings Are a Method for Developing a Reputation among

Fellow Real Estate Salespersons. The successful listor also develops a reputation among fellow real estate salespersons. Associates come for assistance and colistings to the listor who puts merchandise on the market.

"Listing is the backbone of the business. Without listings, you're really not much of a real estate salesperson," comments sales associate Rick Niday of Iowa Reality Company, whose sold listings in 1976 alone exceeded $2 million.

"I am prouder of my listings than of my sales because without listings, without merchandise on the shelves, we do not have anything to sell. I have more respect for somebody who goes out and gets a lot of listings so we can sell them than for the salesperson who comes in and sells our listings and does not bring anything back to the company.

"Listings are most important, and the listor warrants the most respect."

10. Listings Provide Management Training. The successful listor develops skills that are required in managerial and ownership positions.

11. Listings Are a Surer Source of Income during a Depressed Market. When the economy of a community is depressed, the listor usually suffers less than the person who merely sells real estate. Real estate salepersons who confine themselves to selling have only a few buyers with whom to work. Listors of Exclusive Listings, on the other hand, have hundreds of salespeople working for them to sell their listings.

A case in point is that of Sarah Catherine Holley, a sales associate of Sandra Townsend Realty, Charlotte, North Carolina. Sarah has decided never to maintain more or less than 15 listings at a time. "I won't take one on until another moves out of position, so to speak, and this gives me an incentive to get them each sold so I can service more." During January 1977, $250,000 of Sarah's listings in the $30,000 to $40,000 range were sold. At that time some 2,800 houses in her community were for sale in a depressed "buyer's market."

Real estate is one of our nation's largest industries. Fantastic opportunies abound for the 965,815 salespersons and the 593,782 brokers licensed in 1975 (949,757 and 553,313, respectively, in 1974).

Despite the great possibilities, a survey of the National Association of Realtors® disclosed that of the full-time salespeople who responded, over two thirds (69.3 percent) had incomes of less than $20,000 in 1974. Less than 5 percent earned over $50,000 a year.

And those earning below $20,000 were not all first-year associates, as the figures in Table 1–1 reveal.

TABLE 1–1
Median Income of Full-Time REALTOR®–ASSOCIATES by Number of Years in Real Estate Business (1974)

Years in Real Estate	Median Income	Mid–50 Percent Range
1	$ 3,400	$ 1,600– 6,000
2	8,000	4,500–12,000
3	11,000	7,500–15,800
4	12,000	8,000–18,000
5	15,000	8,000–20,500
6–10	17,000	9,600–25,000
11–15	19,300	12,000–28,800
16–25	20,000	9,800–30,000
26–39	18,800	10,000–38,000
40 or more	*	*
All full-time associates	$12,000	$ 7,200–20,000

*Insufficient reports.

The reasons for the poor performance are varied. Nevertheless, anyone long in the business will quickly agree that to be a success, you do what failures don't like to do. And one thing that "failures" generally do not like to do, or cannot seem to do, is list. Even some of those who fell within the upper levels of the surveyed group have been known to envy the seeming magic of the listing giants.

Thus, Charles V. Howe, GRI, past president of Multiple Listing Service and an associate of Smith, Bell and Thompson, Burlington, Vermont, states, "One point I think should be singled out, namely, that although there are so many tapes and books on selling, there is not enough emphasis on listing!"

It is hoped that you will find the following chapters profitable.

But remember, you will find no magic formulas here. You may not even discover anything new. All that this book purports to do is to share with you the methods that top listing producers have *consistently* and *persistently* used to achieve success.

2

Prospecting

It was Saturday, 9:30 A.M. On that morning, for the very first time, I went out into the world knocking on doors as a real estate salesperson —in fact, it was the first time I had done anything "in public" as a real estate salesperson.

I began on the 800 block of Pontiac and had worked my way along the east side of the street up through the 1300 block. When I stopped at 12:30, I had knocked on 42 doors and measured the insides of two houses. The following day an owner who had not been home Saturday morning phoned and asked me to return and evaluate his property.

From those three "leads," I obtained two listings. One was a single-family residence for $27,000. The other was a single-family residence with a run-down, eight-unit, 80-year-old apartment at the back of the lot. This house-apartment combination listed for $107,000. Six months after it sold, I relisted the complex for the new owner for $114,000.

As a result of knocking on 42 doors for three hours, I listed $134,000 in real estate. If the relisting of the house-apartment is included, then my three hours of canvassing generated nearly a quarter of a million dollars in business.

One point I must make now, a point to which we will return later, is that I knocked on 42 doors. I did not talk with 42 homeowners. From one third to one half of the occupants were not at home. One of them was the owner of the house and the apartment.

THE DEBATE REGARDING CANVASSING

A rather vehement debate rages among real estate salespersons over whether one should prospect for listings by canvassing door to door.

Some consider canvassing unprofessional. "Have you ever seen a lawyer or physician going from door to door in search of business?"

Others consider canvassing demeaning. They regard it as begging. Canvassing is inconsistent with the image they have or want to have of themselves, and wish to project to others. And it is depressing to know when you roll out of bed in the morning that you must pound on one door after another, ring bell after bell, *ask, ask, ask,* and hear *no, no, no.*

"I am scared," one real-estate salesperson admits. "I don't know what will happen, what people will say. I don't want a door slammed in my face. I don't want to be hollered at."

Still others believe canvassing to be a waste of time. Calculate, they say, how many phone calls a person can make during the time that another person is knocking on doors. And the canvasser is not certain that anyone will be at home—or that the occupant owns the house. These people believe that in canvassing too much effort is expended for the results obtained and that canvassing does not produce business quickly enough. Such persons would "rather work smarter than harder."

WHY CANVASS?

Those who favor door-to-door canvassing contend that the foregoing objections are, for the most part, symptomatic of a misunderstanding of this method of obtaining listings. "They simply do not know how to go about it."

"I know, and I think it can be documented, that, properly done, door-to-door canvassing is very effective," comments Howard Lubow of Lubow Realty Company, Dayton, Ohio. "Some of the highest paid producers in the country use canvassing as their prime method.

"But it depends on how you do it. You can do anything in such a manner as to have no results. I remember a salesman called on me once, knocking on the door, and said, 'You don't want to buy a storm door, do you?'

"I think he was a salesman. But, of course, he didn't sell me a storm door."

One advantage of door-to-door canvassing is that you can measure what you have done over any given period on any given day. If you decide that you are going to knock on 25 or 50 doors each and every day, regardless of what you may do, you can measure whether or not you have done at least that.

Those in the business know how easy it is to become involved in minutiae, to "piddle around with paperwork." Paperwork, phone calls, errands, and problem solving are all important. But it is a question of priorities. Competent real estate salespersons have knowledge and service to sell. Their worth is in their brain and in their tongue, not in doing typing with their hands, in running errands with their legs, or in lending their ears to the problems of their associates.

Canvassing also enables salespersons to know the neighborhood in which they intend to work. They can visually determine the condition of the area and the houses, if any, which are for sale. They have a chance to discover the clues that indicate possible real estate activity.

Being knowledgeable about which houses have sold and about their prices, condition, and location in the neighborhood gives the real estate salesperson self-confidence and impresses prospects and clients.

Speaking face-to-face with homeowners and tenants is an easy way to obtain leads of immediate or eventual listings.

"It's amazing that on any particular street you can usually find somebody who knows what's going on on the whole street," insists Dave McGinnis of Jones and Jacob, Inc., South Burlington, Vermont. "You'll just come upon the right house, and the housewife, or whoever is there, can tell you what is going on in the neighborhood or on the street. So it's not a hard process. I usually find out what I'm looking for after knocking on a couple of doors."

And if you present a reasonably neat and pleasant appearance, people will be more receptive to you than they will be to a blind phone call or an unsolicited letter. Canvassing regularly will wipe away the smear of "stranger."

Canvassing should not be considered unprofessional. "Professional" merely means being paid for what you do. In that light, no one wants to be unprofessional. Of course, what the opponents of canvassing really mean is that they think canvassing is undignified. But that is mainly a frame of mind, an interior attitude.

There is nothing undignified about working at your place of business. Ballplayers belong on the field. Physicians belong where sick people are, in the hospital and the clinic. Attorneys function best in the courtroom or their office library. And real estate salespersons belong with their product—houses, land, buildings. That is their marketplace.

Not one minute is wasted by the salesperson who knows how to canvass properly. Whether or not an occupant is home is not entirely relevant. You have learned about the houses. You develop a feeling about the neighborhood which will give you knowledge and a sense of ease. And if you use the correct methods, those away from home will know you were there. With the correct methods, you need never experience any apprehension or fear, or feel that you are begging. And with the correct methods, canvassing is a source of many listings and consequently a method for earning a good living.

Trivial as it may sound, canvassing affords an opportunity for exercise. Time is at a premium for successful salespersons. Often they do not have time for regular exercise. Getting out and walking while working furnishes them with at least some physical activity.

Canvassing is an integral, indispensable part of an effective listing program. As suggested before, it not only enables you and the people to meet one another "eyeball to eyeball," but it also permits you to become acquainted with different areas.

WHERE TO PROSPECT?

Gary Shapiro, now of Price/Shapiro Realtors®, Inc., and formerly a consistent top producer and lifetime Million Dollar Club member of Fannin Realty, Scottsdale, Arizona, relates that when he began in the business he had no referrals. "I knocked on doors. I didn't pick any specific area. I scattered my shot, in that I went where there was currently some activity. For instance, if I had sold something in a given neighborhood, I would go back to the rest of the neighborhood. I did not adopt a specific area."

If she were to advise salespersons on how to begin getting listings, Lucy Ann Bell would recommend that they "ring doorbells. And once you get a listing, contact all the neighbors on the block. That's how I built up my business."

Ray Novotny of Bermel Smaby Realty, Minneapolis, explains, "Actually, when I do go out cold-calling, it's really not *cold* calling. It's all predetermined. I look at a block and calculate, 'There three homes sold last year, and three homes sold the year before.' In an area where people sell every four or five years, that means there are some great potential candidates for listings this coming year.

"I check my multiple listing books and my records. If a house sold last year, the owner isn't likely to sell this year. But somebody who's been in a home for three years may be getting tired of the place. That's a prospect."

Prospecting for Rosamond Shaw of Robert Bruce Realty, Philadelphia, is "simply a matter of common sense. Sit down and think. Who's likely to sell? And why? And then work on that."

Among his methods of finding out who is likely to sell, top producer Earl M. Richardson of Jack Conway & Co., Boston, hunts for boats for sale.

"This is a big thing with me. Along the ocean here we have quite a few marinas. I find a boat for sale with a phone number on it. So I call that number, and a lot of times I'll find there's a house that'll be coming up for sale."

Richardson will go anywhere to ferret out a listing. For example, in checking out vacant houses, another of his methods, Earl came across a fine antique property in Duxbury. He went to the town hall and determined the name and address of the person to whom the tax bill was being sent. Instead of telephoning the owners, Earl got his car, made a five-hour drive to Portland, Maine, located the owners, knocked on their door, and identified himself.

"Needless to say, they were quite impressed. I found out while I was there that they had already had four telephone calls from other brokers on the same house. But I was the only one who appeared in person. And when I walked away, I had an exclusive listing for six months. I sold the house shortly thereafter.

"And that's the way I do it. But you won't find too many people who will. It's a carry-over from 30 years' experience in the Army: being prompt, hard work, tireless effort. I'm up every morning at 5:30. I go out many mornings just to look at new houses being built." Earl also uses those early morning hours to check *"For Sale by Owner"* newspaper ads and empty houses.

"Along those same lines, of course, I keep in constant touch with my milkman to find out whether any of the customers on his route are cutting their delivery off, because they might be moving. That gives me leads. I also check with my mailman.

"I just continually ask them, 'Do you know anyone who is about to move?' They tell me, and I go right over there and ask the owners whether they are interested in selling their property. I've picked up lots of listings that way.

"The accent in my approach is directness. I think that's why I've been successful in listing. Talking with people personally rather than over the telephone."

Another real estate salesperson who "percolates and circulates" (to cite the advice of Mrs. Lee Burch of Ludlow, Inc., Indianapolis) is Mivy Harring of Geer Real Estate Co., Kansas City, Kansas.

Mrs. Harring finds that she is most effective approaching people face-to-face. She is particularly effective on Saturday mornings when the weather is good and people are out working in their yards.

"Real estate is a people business. The personal approach—seeing each other face-to-face, seeing what we each look like, seeing what kinds of persons we each are—this, I think, has had a lot to do with my success."

Mivy, like Earl Richardson, hunts for vacant houses. She also hunts for houses in which curtains are coming down or painting or repairing is going on. "Many times, seeing curtains down, I've knocked on the door only to be told, 'Oh, no. We're just cleaning.' But the contact is never a waste of time."

Mrs. Harring's son, with his employer's permission, distributes her personalized pens to customers after they sign their credit card for the gas and oil they purchase. This gesture adds to the activity of the station and Mivy's source of leads.

With so much competition, "you try to be the first to get to owners," Mivy points out. "The only way you can do that is by scanning the newspapers and keeping abreast of what's happening in the community. A friend in the moving business has been keeping me informed of activity and of anticipated traffic."

Mivy also takes advantage of the activity which develops at nearby Fort Leavenworth. "I've learned to know at what times of the year military personnel will be transferred. For example, Fort Leavenworth has Command General Staff College, which runs until the beginning of June. Therefore, I know that the majority of people will be putting their houses on the market in advance of this June move."

Such movements of military personnel can, of course, be analyzed anywhere in the country. Mrs. Harring identifies these people through the use of her personal copies of R. L. Polk's *City Directory*.

FIGURE 2–1
The *City Directory's* White Pages

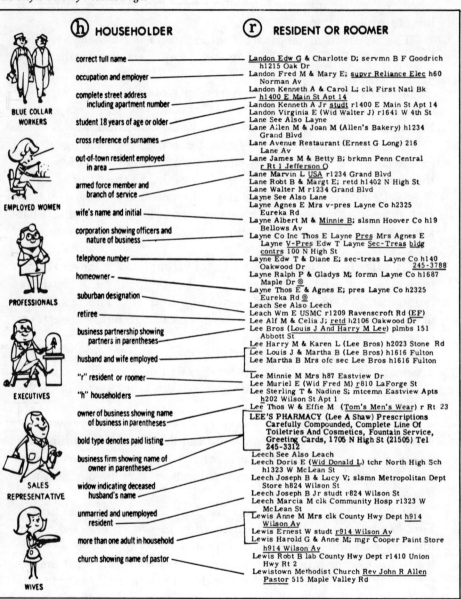

THE CITY DIRECTORY

Since top producers seem to be aquainted with the use of this *Directory,* whereas *great numbers of others are unaware of its "se-*

FIGURE 2–2
The *City Directory's* **Green Pages**

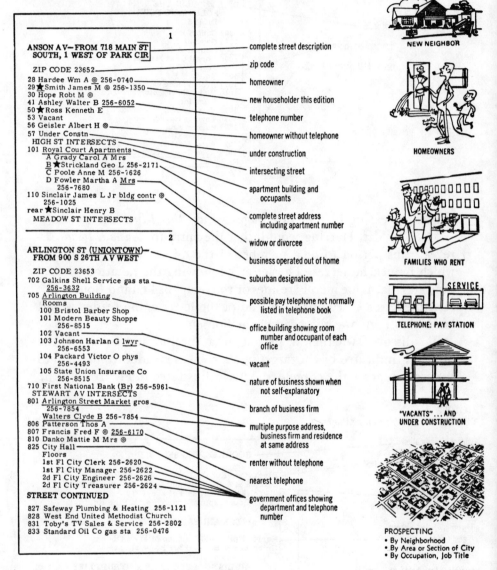

◎ HOMEOWNER SYMBOL   ★ NEW NEIGHBOR SYMBOL

1

ANSON AV—FROM 718 MAIN ST
SOUTH, 1 WEST OF PARK CIR ——— complete street description

ZIP CODE 23652 ——— zip code

28 Hardee Wm A ◎ 256-0740 ——— homeowner
29 ★Smith James M ◎ 256-1350 —
30 Hope Robt M ◎
41 Ashley Walter B 256-6052 ——— new householder this edition
50 ★Ross Kenneth E
53 Vacant ——— telephone number
56 Geisler Albert H ◎ —
57 Under Constn ——— homeowner without telephone
HIGH ST INTERSECTS —
101 Royal Court Apartments ——— under construction
  A Grady Carol A Mrs
  B ★Strickland Geo L 256-2171 ——— intersecting street
  C Poole Anne M 256-7626
  D Fowler Martha A Mrs ——— apartment building and
    256-7680   occupants
110 Sinclair James L Jr bldg contr ◎
  256-1025 ——— complete street address
rear ★Sinclair Henry B   including apartment number
  MEADOW ST INTERSECTS

2

ARLINGTON ST (UNIONTOWN)—
FROM 900 S 26TH AV WEST ——— widow or divorcee

ZIP CODE 23653 ——— business operated out of home

702 Galkins Shell Service gas sta ——— suburban designation
  256-3632
705 Arlington Building ——— possible pay telephone not normally
  Rooms   listed in telephone book
  100 Bristol Barber Shop
  101 Modern Beauty Shoppe
    256-8515 ——— office building showing room
  102 Vacant   number and occupant of each
  103 Johnson Harlan G lwyr   office
    256-6553
  104 Packard Victor O phys ——— vacant
    256-4493
  105 State Union Insurance Co
    256-8515 ——— nature of business shown when
710 First National Bank (Br) 256-5961   not self-explanatory
STEWART AV INTERSECTS
801 Arlington Street Market gros ——— branch of business firm
  256-7854
  Walters Clyde B 256-7854 —
806 Patterson Thos A
807 Francis Fred F ◎ 256-6170 ——— multiple purpose address,
810 Danko Mattie M Mrs ◎   business firm and residence
825 City Hall   at same address
  Floors
  1st Fl City Clerk 256-2620 ——— renter without telephone
  1st Fl City Manager 256-2622
  2d Fl City Engineer 256-2626 ——— nearest telephone
  2d Fl City Treasurer 256-2624
STREET CONTINUED ——— government offices showing
                              department and telephone
827 Safeway Plumbing & Heating 256-1121   number
828 West End United Methodist Church
831 Toby's TV Sales & Service 256-2802
833 Standard Oil Co gas sta 256-0476

NEW NEIGHBOR

HOMEOWNERS

FAMILIES WHO RENT

SERVICE

TELEPHONE: PAY STATION

"VACANTS"...AND
UNDER CONSTRUCTION

PROSPECTING
• By Neighborhood
• By Area or Section of City
• By Occupation, Job Title

crets", it is worthwhile to point out some of the information in this indispensable tool.

The *Directory* is divided into several color-coded sections.

By referring to Figure 2–1, you may see an illustration of types of

14

FIGURE 2-3
The *City Directory's* Blue Pages

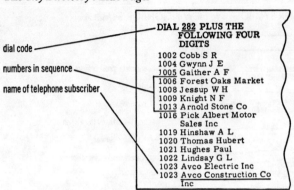

dial code

numbers in sequence

name of telephone subscriber

DIAL **282** PLUS THE
FOLLOWING FOUR
DIGITS
1002 Cobb S R
1004 Gwynn J E
1005 Gaither A F
1006 Forest Oaks Market
1008 Jessup W H
1009 Knight N F
1013 Arnold Stone Co
1016 Pick Albert Motor
Sales Inc
1019 Hinshaw A L
1020 Thomas Hubert
1021 Hughes Paul
1022 Lindsay G L
1023 Avco Electric Inc
1023 Avco Construction Co
Inc

entries appearing in its *white pages*. Study *this illustration closely*.

Note, as Mrs. Harring would, that the entry for *Lane, Marvin L.* reveals this person to be a member of the military and discloses in which branch he serves. The letter *r* following the notation "USA" indicates that Lane merely resides or rooms at 1234 Grand Boulevard. Had the letter *h* been used instead of the letter *r*, the reader would know that Lane was the head of the household.

To discover whether a person at a specific address *owns* the property (indicated by the target symbol ⊙), the reader would turn to the *green pages* of the *Directory*. This is illustrated in Figure 2.2. The

FIGURE 2-4
The *City Directory's* Yellow Pages

business classification

complete name and street address

professional style extended
information listing
includes telephone numbers

all firms are listed without
cost under their
principal classification

heavy black type (bold type listing)
denotes paid listing

additional reference to
customers' advertisements

suburban designation

BOOKKEEPING SERVICE

Blackstone Ronald J 310 College St Rm 101
Dixon J E & Co Suite 600 Dix Bldg 125 S Maple St
Tel 282-1675 Res Tel 285-6972
Local Bookkeeping Service 642 E Pine Rd

BOX MANUFACTURERS

Karton Box Co 142 Bishop Mill Rd (RV)
Union Box & Bag Inc 301 Ragsdale St

BUILDING MATERIALS AND SUPPLIES

GOLDSTONE BUILDERS SUPPLY INC, 1645
Battle Av, PO Box 7549, Anytown, USA (27840)
Tel 285-1849 (See Index To Advertisers)
Hedgewood Home & Building Supply Co 401
Jamesville Rd
Nelte Lumber & Building Materials 525 Adams
Rd (TC)

new neighbor symbol ★ identifies a person whose occupancy of the premises began after the previous year's *Directory* was published.

Figure 2–3 shows examples of the telephone entries that appear in the *blue pages*. In this section, telephone numbers are listed in numerical sequence.

Figure 2–4 illustrates the information contained in the *yellow pages*. This section lists businesses according to type. It also includes every professional, club, society, association, hospital, cemetery, labor organization, library, park, playground, and school. The yellow pages of the *Directory* may contain the only complete classification of the businesses in a community.

Subscribers of the *Directory* are entitled to certain services. Among these is the privilege of obtaining an *update* of information from the *Directory's* local library. In most cities the library also maintains volumes of out-of-town directories. Should the local community not be large enough to accomodate a complete libary of directories, the subscriber may ask the local *City Directory* librarian to obtain the particular information desired.

Information for the *Directory* is obtained by a house-to-house canvass. Other valuable services available to the real estate salesperson from R. C. Polk and Company will be discussed later.

ADDITIONAL SOURCES

The consensus of the top producers is expressed by James Kunkel of S. J. Pounder Realty Company, Portland, Oregon, when he says he is always "thinking real estate. And meeting people. You've got to see and meet people. And don't be afraid to talk to them."

Eunice S. Reass is now manager of the Residential Division of Laguarta, Gavrel & Kirk, Inc., Houston. Before she assumed her present position, no one was able to match her performance as a listor in the city. At least $2 million of her listings were sold every year. At one time Eunice set herself the goal of getting her first $1 million of listings sold by May 15. Then she moved her goal forward to May 1, and then to April 15.

In accordance with Jim Kundel's comments, Eunice Reass asserts that "the problem with most salespeople is that they don't realize that wherever they go they're salespeople. Whether they are going to a dinner dance or to the opera, they carry their cards with them at all times.

"No matter where you go, people are speaking about real estate. If you sit down in a drugstore and listen to what's going on at the next table, I'm willing to bet that five times out of six the people are talking about houses. It's a favorite topic of conversation.

"I remember seeing a person looking at a newspaper, reading the 'Houses for Sale' columns. I walked over, put my card down, and asked if I could help."

And, of course, this is one of the advantages a real estate salesperson has over other types of salespersons: almost everyone is interested in and enjoys talking about real estate.

Ruth Hubbard, Million Dollar salesperson for Grempler Reality, Baltimore, noted that whereas she rang doorbells when she began, real estate salespersons are now prohibited from cold-canvassing. "We really can't even solicit people in the paper anymore."

Prospecting, then, involves going from relatives to next-door neighbors to milkmen to bankers to your school to your churches. "Quite simply, just ask, 'Do you know anyone who wants to sell any real estate?' And give out your business cards, of course. 'I'm in real estate, and I'm really trying to build a business. I need your help.' I have built my business that way. But nobody told me these things," says Ms. Hubbard.

Speaking of prospecting through the schools, top producer Mike Beaton of Schweitzer Real Estate Co., Grosse Point, Michigan, tells about the real estate salesperson who "very effectively in a tight-knit community uses her school-age children as a source of finding out from the grapevine when parents are thinking about and discussing a move. She gets advance notice that way and finds it a very effective way of getting listings."

Nila R. Laman, sales associate of Jack Matthews and Co., Las Vegas, was the secretary for the Western High School Rooters Club. "And I had a fantastic thing going there. I probably sold a house to every kid who graduated and got married. Then, when the kids left, I listed and sold their parents' big empty houses and got them little houses, and on and on."

Joyce Steffen, top producer for the past six years for Robedeaux, Inc., Milwaukee, uses another bird-dogging method. Joyce benefits from the fact that her husband has his own tax consultant business. When corresponding with clients, Mr. Steffen includes his wife's business card. Joyce gets many listings from these clients. "They just tell us, 'Well, next year we are selling.' "

And Mrs. Burch secures a lot of listing business by prospecting for leads among agents in the various commercial real estate departments in her city. They advise her of forthcoming business activities that will effect listings.

Colleen R. Rosinbum of Seattle, Washington, who is one of the country's top 25 salespeople for Coldwell Banker, has cold-canvassed door to door as a part of her listing program. To illustrate the effectiveness of this method, Colleen described what happened when a woman whom she reached in this way asked for a market analysis on a house which the woman was renting to students for $300 a month. It turned out that the house was worth $60,000.

At that time the woman was not interested in listing, but only curious about the value of her rental property. Mrs. Rosinbum left the valuation with her, sensing that this might lead to a listing.

About two months later, while showing a client homes, Colleen drove by the house and pointed it out to the client. He told her to stop the car. He hopped out, walked about the outside of the home, got back in the car, and made an offer without waiting to see the inside.

Naturally the woman was shocked when Ms. Rosinbum brought the offer to her. When Colleen pointed out that the woman was losing money, the woman asked Colleen to show her how she could do better. After an explanation, the woman agreed to let Colleen list and sell the rental house to the client. The woman bought another property with the proceeds.

Not long after that transaction, the woman phoned Ms. Rosinbum and told her that the house next door was being rented and that the occupants were driving her crazy. Colleen contacted the landlord, listed his house, and then sold it to the woman.

About four weeks later the woman called Colleen and said that she wanted to buy another property. Colleen set to work again and located what the woman wanted.

All in all, Colleen realized two listings and five sales as a result of her prospecting effort.

Although his company prefers not to handle rentals, Charles Howe has used advertisements in the "Wanted to Rent" column with the message, "Let us handle your rental property for you."

His objective, of course, is to obtain listings. His idea is that the owners will eventually elect to sell and will give the listing to him.

As an example of the responses to his ad, Howe cited a house that he was given to rent until the owners, a couple retiring to the South, were certain that they could find the home they wanted in the new location, at which time they would sell their Vermont home.

Advertising about his performance that his company puts in newspapers has been a source of listings for Bruce Jorgensen. "I get people calling me, saying, 'I saw your picture in the paper because you are doing a good job.' "

The author has found that sellers and prospective sellers religiously read the ads, and that an effective way to impress them with his listing activity is to occasionally group several of his listings into a display ad in the classified section for a certain area within the community. (A sample appears in Figure 2–5.)

Expired listings are a source of business for many top producers, such as Mike Knapp of Iowa Reality, Des Moines.

In some areas of the nation, the multiple listing service (MLS) publishes the beginning and expiration dates of the listing period for each property. Having shown these properties while they were listed with another broker, real estate salespersons are in a position to analyze why they were not sold. The day after an expiration, they can be prepared to approach the owner with a view to listing it themselves.

In areas of the country where the MLS book does not provide the listing dates, real estate salespersons can estimate such information. By retaining their MLS books, they have the approximate date when a listing begins, since most multiple listing boards require that the entry appear in multilist within a specified period of time from the date the listing is taken. Moreover, each entry is generally assigned a sequence number, which will again reflect when the property came on the market. If listings in a given community are customarily taken for 120 days, real estate salesperson can gauge the date of expiration and be prepared to solicit an expired listing.

The advantage of contacting the owners of such homes lies in the fact that there is an urgency to sell. "You know," says Mike, "that the person wants to sell this home right now."

Tax rolls and information from the county assessor's office enable many of the million- and multi-million-dollar listors to obtain new listings. As will be discussed later, through the use of these public records, the listor can identify which properties are rental, who owns them, and when the investor is likely to be willing to sell.

FIGURE 2–5
Advertising to Attract Sellers

EXCEPTIONAL PARK-HILL
Beautiful 6 bdrm., contemporary on 5 lots. 4 baths, family room, hot water heat, and everything else you need and ever wanted.

JUST LISTED
This has to be one of the most beautiful 3 + 1 bdrm. ranch-style homes in the Hilltop-Crestmoor area. Among the limitless features are a gorgeous living room with fireplace, spacious formal dining room, breakfast room off a beautiful, bright, new fully equipped kitchen, 2 baths, bsmt., 2 car detached garage, automatic sprinkler system and on and on.

FOR THE SHREWD AND WISE
Let the one bdrm. apt. at the rear of this property make the payments on this 2 story 3 bdrm. home which has been remodeled. Fireplace and dining room.

1053 POPLAR
This home has everything! 2 bdrms., dining room, family room with fireplace, 2 car garage, gorgeous yard. Out of town owner wants action!

QUALITY HOUSE
1325 Fairfax is a Tudor-style home with 2 + 2 bdrms., featuring 2 fireplaces, formal dining room, 1 3/4 baths, full finished bsmt., 2 car garage.

1117 PONTIAC
3 bdrms., covered patio, carpeted. Move right in—perfect condition.

FIRST TIME OFFERED
3001 E. 34th Ave. 2 bdrms., attractive well kept home. Priced right. Be the first to see it.

CALL PETE WIGGINTON
572-1228

TheMooreWay REALTOR

Another method of using the public records to prospect for likely leads is described by Eileen Wallen of New Orleans. "In the uptown, university section of New Orleans, an older, well-established area is undergoing transition because aging owners need to sell off the property they have lived in for many, many years." By analyzing the public records, the length of ownership, the age of the owners, and the likelihood of obtaining listings can be determined.

The top listors incessantly emphasize the point made by Carolyn Rosen-Miller, president of Carolyn Rosen Riteway, Miami, Florida. "We want our salespeople to contact everyone in their sphere of influence. That means anyone they know. We want them to be persistent and to let those people know they are in the real estate business. 'Do you know anyone who might possibly be interested in selling?' We tell our salespeople to leave their cards wherever they go, whether it is to the gas station, to the beauty parlor, out for lunch, or out to dinner. 'I am in the real estate business and associated with Riteway. And I would like to help you with any real estate matters you may have. Feel free to consult me about anything—if you have a question about property taxes, or schools, or whatever.' "

Like other top listors, Carolyn's listors work with a lot of builders —a big source of listings everywhere.

Uncanny as it may seem, wherever one "For Sale" sign goes up, listors long in the business know that invariably one or more other sale signs will soon sprout up in the vicinity (on the same block or on an adjoining block). It does not matter whether the sign is put up by an owner or by a real estate salesperson. By referring to the multi-list entries or just by driving through areas he or she prefers, the listor who uses the proper approach can generate many additional listings.

3

For Sale by Owner

The owner who erects his own "For Sale" sign has said "no" to the real estate salesperson even before the salesperson gets to the owner's front door.

This fact scares off many real estate salespersons. But not the "heavyweights."

WHY BOTHER WITH THEM?

"FSBOs" are my big bag," declares Mike Beaton.

"That's where the business is," exults David Webster, GRI, of Gifford Reality, Norfolk, Virginia. "If you've got FSBOs, you know they have an interest in selling their property. There is no doubt about that.

"If I moved to a new area where I didn't know anybody, I would take the paper each morning and circle the 'For Sale by Owner' ads and make sure I contacted each FSBO. In our area, we have anywhere from three to ten new ones every day.

"I know these people want to sell that property. And if they can't sell it themselves, I can sell it for them. And I do."

According to Maurice Johnson, associate broker of Batt and Miller, Reality One, Buffalo, New York, "The 'For Sale by Owner' is a number one source of listings, especially for someone new in the business or in the community. This business is quick and ready and on the market."

"Because you do have to be sharper than the next person in order to get a 'For Sale by Owner,' it is a real proving ground," says Mrs. Burch. "Nevertheless, it's an excellent source of business. That's the way I got started in real estate." And it's a method she still pursues even after 20 years in the business and many referrals.

WHAT SYSTEM?

"One of my associates, one of the most successful in the business, gets up at 6:30 every morning, circles all the 'For Sale by Owner' advertisements, and makes certain to see as many FSBOs as he can that day," says Dave Webster.

After reading the ads, Mike Beaton identifies the names of owners with addresses in his crisscross directory. ("If you are going to call on FSBOs, you must call them by name," notes Mrs. Burch.)

Beaton phones the owners, then follows up with letters stating the benefits of using professional services, describing his company, and detailing his individual credentials. He places a card for each owner in his active file. "I start mailing letters to the owners and may phone once or several times. Eventually, if I don't achieve anything with the phone calls, I go out and see them personally."

Mrs. Burch maintains a separate book of FSBOs in which she records everything pertaining to them: the dates on which she contacts them, where and why they are moving, when they advertise, and so forth.

THE APPROACH BY PHONE

Mike Beaton approaches FSBOs by phone. He believes that volume is the key. Make enough contacts, and eventually you will reach someone who wants to talk with a real estate salesperson.

"When I phone I identify myself and ask permission to talk to them, stating that I'd like to get together to explain a marketing program that will enable them to sell their property for top dollar. 'Could we get together tonight about ten minutes to eight, or would tomorrow evening at 7:50 be better for you?' And it's that simple."

Colleen Rosinbum also values the phone approach to making appointments with FSBOs. "Of course, it's helpful to be first. And to make them feel comfortable. But telephone manner is important.

"Certainly there are some who are difficult. But mainly the response is good. Most of the owners are interested in talking with someone about the price they have put on their home."

When calling, Colleen first identifies herself. She continues by remarking, "I see you are selling your home. How are you doing?" Then she asks a few questions about the house. "It sounds attractive. I'd like to come out and see it."

"Try to get the appointment to see the house," says Collen. "Once they have committed themselves to allow you to come see the house, you are pretty much on your way. Just get that appointment!"

With those owners whose first response is, "Well, no, I don't think so," Colleen continues to talk. Then, again, she will persist with, "I'd like to come out and talk with you about marketing your property. I have some very good ideas about it. I'll be out at [such and such a time]."

Colleen does not use a prepared speech. "I think that comes off as phony."

THE APPROACH IN PERSON

Byron Dennis, a top listor and the manager of Bourne-McGehee Realtors®, Jackson, Mississippi, approaches the owner directly after seeing a sign in the yard or an ad in the paper. "The first time is low-key. 'How are you doing? Are you having a lot of people just looking?' "

"I try to do all my business in person," says Dave Webster. "I approach the FSBOs low-key. I stop by to find out what they are doing, what they know and don't know. Usually I leave my card and some information that would help them.

"When I knock on that door I'm really there to do just exactly what I said. I'm not trying to get a listing on the first visit. A lot of people blow it the first time. When they go in, they try to button-down the listing the first time. I don't do that. I'm only there to offer my services to those people."

On the other hand, after Earl Richardson, who has a goal of eight listings per week, obtains the necessary information about the owner and the property, he goes right to the property prepared to take the listing.

"I've got a sign with me and my lockbox. I carry my listing agreement all made out. The price was in the paper—that's their sales price. I put our commission on top of that. So that when I go out to talk with them, I've got everything ready, in hand, in a folder.

"I find I have much better luck confronting them face-to-face. It is very easy on the phone to say, 'We're not interested. We are going to sell it ourselves.'

"I hand the owner my card and say, 'I'm Earl Richardson from Jack Conway Real Estate Company. I understand your home is for sale. I have a program here I'd like to talk to you about.' I have been refused many times, but I've been successful more times, particularly if the seller is in a hurry because of relocation or the like."

Mrs. Burch also notes the importance of identifying the selling motive. "FSBOs are of two kinds. There are those who list their house and are in a hurry. Perhaps the husband has gone away and the wife is there by herself, and hating every minute of it. She will usually go along with the idea of getting her husband sold on the idea of listing it. There are other people, such as the ones who say, 'We've sold our house before. We don't need any help.'

"I try to figure out which is the A seller and which is the B seller. I work on the A. It all depends on motivation."

Dave McGinnis agrees that determining the sincerity of the sellers is important. "I like to find out why they are selling. If they're just trying to shoot for a high figure, I don't spend any time on them. But if I've got an individual who has bought another home or has been transferred, then I spend my time."

Joyce Steffen tries various approaches, according to the type of person she encounters. "You almost need to change your personality to fit the situation. Some are receptive; some are very cold. It is necessary to at least get them to smile. You cannot be pushy."

And you must identify their problem. "I remember when I went out and looked for a car," Joyce relates. "The first thing the salesman said was, 'You really should buy this car. It's your color.' That turned me off. I was interested in buying a car—not a color."

Joyce returned the next night and bought a car from a salesman who listened to what she wanted in the way of price, style, and features, and offered her a choice among three automobiles.

Maurice Johnson stresses an effective question every real estate salesperson should get in the habit of using: "Apparently you must have some reason for feeling that way." It gets results.

"Last night I made a cold call on FSBOs on Homestead Drive. I didn't know the people. I got the lead from an ad in the paper. I went over, knocked on the door, and introduced myself. 'Good evening, my name is Maurey Johnson. I'm with Batt and Miller Real Estate. I noticed you have an ad in the paper to sell your home. And I'm wondering if I could be of service to you.'

"Ninety-nine percent of the time they're going to say 'no,' just as she did. But to this I countered, 'Apparently you must have some reason for feeling that way.' And she replied, 'Wait just a second.' "

The woman got her husband. After Maurey repeated his remarks, the husband let him in. His question not only gained him entry, but also identified the person from whom he needed to obtain a decision.

Most of the top listors agree with Mrs. Burch's emphasis on the importance of being courteous and sincere, of expressing an interest in the FSBO's home, and of developing rapport.

Mrs. Burch explains, "After I knock on the door I say, 'I see you are selling your house yourself, and I don't blame you at all. I would probably do the same. But if after you try it awhile you discover that you need help, please call me. If you need the answer to *any* question, give me a ring.'

"The one leading question that has made my dollars is, 'Would you object to my looking at your house?' And very few people will object to your looking.

"If you are pleasant and kind and friendly, you don't have any problem. And you have got to get acquainted with people. Of course, it's difficult to get acquainted with a door in between, but if you say something kind and you offer your card, which requires them to open the door, it is very easy to get in."

Rosemary Kane, a top listor for Dayton Cople Realty's Waianae office in Honolulu, uses this approach, "I give the FSBOs a general rundown on what has sold in the area, and what I feel is happening to the area in general that will enhance their property values. Then I give them a fair market analysis of what I think their property will sell for. And I emphasize what I personally can do for them."

In return for a promise to get the listing, Dave Webster, ordinarily bounces four or five tidbits around until he hits on something the owner did not know. "The first thing you should do is get yourself a professional-looking sign, not any Mickey Mouse sign. And make certain you always have somebody at home to answer the phone and make appointments."

THE FOLLOW-UP

Mike Beaton's mailing program consists of sending a letter once a week for the four weeks following his initial phone contact. His first letter stresses the advantages of his company, points out his individual credentials, and itemizes the benefits of using a professional real estate broker. The second letter zeroes in on the fact that most FSBOs are attempting to save money. In answering the question "Does having a broker pay?" Beaton shows that, in effect, there is no net cost to the owner. His subsequent letters continue to develop the issues raised in letters one and two.

Mrs. Burch, a believer in the two-visit method, uses the first visit to get into the home, become acquainted with one or both of the owners, and find out why the house is being sold. In order to time her visit when children are not present, she shows up at about 10:30 in the morning or 2:30 in the afternoon.

She follows up with a thank-you note and then makes a phone call in four or five days. If the sellers are having an open house, she contacts them to ask, "How are you doing? Are many people showing up?" She may even suggest a rewording of their newspaper advertisement.

"So many times the wife will call me and say, 'Listen, Mrs. Burch, I've talked with my husband, and he really would like to hear what you have to say about selling our house."

"A lot of agents don't follow up," says Webster. "They hit the FSBOs one time and figure that is it. But it isn't. I usually call back in 48 to 72 hours, find out how they are doing, and provide some additional piece of information. Usually this second call lets me know where I stand. The owners will either open up and let me know what they have done, or they will button up."

"If I don't sign them up on the first visit I call on them again as soon as I can. I have a lot of confidence in what I am going to say," remarks Rosemary Kane.

POINTS OF EMPHASIS AND OBJECTIONS

All of the top listors know what salient facts they intend to cover once they are inside the prospects' home. How the material is covered varies all the way from a very structured presentation out of a book to a seemingly off-the-cuff conversation. But certain points must be given special emphasis in dealing with the FSBO.

According to Dave Webster, "One thing the average agent always forgets to say is, 'The service of a real estate broker is completely tax deductible.' The run-of-the-mill salesperson doesn't give any justification for being there at the door other than 'I want the listing,' 'I can do it,' 'I've done it,' ta-da, ta-da, ta-da. The same old rhetoric. After all, these people are paying you a lot of money."

Mike Beaton uses a presentation outline he's prepared which includes credentials about his company and himself, statistical data on what is happening in the community, and industry figures which show that broker-sold properties bring more money.

To illustrate his point, Beaton gave the example of a house he had listed at $45,900. The owners had been willing to accept an offer of $45,000 but were advised against doing so. Because of the showings by different real estate salespersons, a competitive spirit was generated. Buyers and brokers were aware of this activity. The next offer that came in was for $45,500. "There you have competitiveness in the industry forcing the price up. But in the 'For Sale by Owner' situation the seller is in a position to negotiate with only one buyer—and both of them know it."

To the objection "We are not listing with a Realtor® to save the 7 percent commission," Mike normally replies, "That's because money is important to you, Mr. and Mrs. Seller. And that's precisely why you and I should get together. We have a record of selling properties at a price that enables our clients to get the maximum amount for their homes."

Dave McGinnis uses figures, charts, and graphs to show FSBOs how much of the market they can draw upon as compared to the marketing strength available to and generated by the real estate broker.

"I believe that FSBOs generally give away the sales commission anyway by accepting a lower price than they should have accepted," comments Byron Dennis. "I explain that in most cases it doesn't cost them anything to let a real estate broker handle their listing. And I back this claim up by comparing the prices of houses sold by their owners with the prices of like properties sold by real estate brokers."

A standard question Maurice Johnson asks is, "Do you have anyone in mind if you don't sell the house yourself?" A good percentage will answer "no."

Mrs. Burch finds it most helpful to ask the owners how they established the price they are asking.

Dave Webster says, "I approach the sellers in the right frame of mind. I go in with the idea that I'm there to help these people. A lot of salespeople feel that the initial harshnesss expressed by sellers cannot be overcome.

"These people really do need and want our help. But their dilemma is that they think they cannot afford the commission."

It is for this reason that practically all the top listors calculate for the FSBO what net amount will be realized. The gross sales price is, for the most part, irrelevant to the FSBO.

"I want the owners to know realistically the lowest amount they will receive," explains Carole Kelby, a leading listor for Thorsen Realty, Chicago, Illinois. When the correct comparable sales price is determined and when the seller is clearly shown what income tax deductions are available and what costly pitfalls can be avoided and what savings can be realized by a competent real estate broker, the real estate salesperson gets the listing.

Don Jackson of Gifford Realty, Norfolk, Virginia, explains, "Rather than say, 'Mr. Prospect, I just want to stop in and tell you how great I am,' which almost everybody does, many of our associates now say, 'I'd like to show you a short educational film that we have found helps people in circumstances like your own to sell their own home.' "

Jackson is referring to an audiovisual program developed by Practical Sales Training, Inc., Denver. This remarkable selling tool houses a Bell and Howell slide projector and a cassette recorder in a 5½-inch attaché case. The entire unit weighs 20 pounds.

Among the presentations available is one entitled "Mr. Pennywise." Expressly designed for the FSBO, the excellent selling tool does in 15 minutes and 10 seconds what the typical salesperson may require an hour or more to accomplish.

The program's advantages include (1) easing entry into the seller's home, (2) providing an effective and professional presentation, and (3) achieving within 18 minutes an evaluation of whether the seller will list with the real estate salesperson.

A device in the unit enables the salesperson to audit his or her conversation with the prospect in order to permit a subsequent evaluation of the salesperson's presentation.

4

The Locational Farm

In May 1973, Dan Bloomquist became associated with Moore Realty of Colorado. He earned in excess of $50,000 in 1976.

After three years in the real estate business, Donald J. Nourse, a sales-associate specializing in the Irvine Community in the Newport–San Joaquin Hills area of California, ended the Bicentennial year with earnings of some $70,000.

Dan and Don reached their income levels in residential real estate by specializing in a *farm*.

Within a few weeks after he started, Dan Bloomquist began to work a farm of 600 homes in the $30,000 to $45,000 price range. In 1974, he listed 36 percent of all the houses put on the market in his farm area. In 1975, Dan got 49 percent of all the listing business in his area. Don Nourse obtained similar results.

WHAT IS IT?

The *farm* concept is common knowledge among real estate sales-persons—or should be.

Since the term *farm* as used in real estate selling can refer to a group of people having some common denominator of relationship or to a group of houses within a specific geographic area, the distinction will be made between a *locational farm* and an *associational farm*. The latter will be discussed in the next chapter.

WHY HAVE ONE?

Bloomquist describes the advantages of having a farm as follows: "You develop security by working a farm. You can *count* on it as a source of income. You'll also find it a much easier way to beat the competition. And you can count on it as a source of leads. You'll find that homeowners will refer people from outside your area to you. For example, when someone moves to town, they will advise that person to contact you."

Eunice Reass recalls that she used a farm to get started in a new community. "When we moved to Houston from New England 15 years ago, I knew only one or two people with my husband's firm. And I joined a real estate company which at that time was brand-new.

"But I concentrated on farming one area. At that time, when house prices averaged about $45,000, I called myself the $20,000 expert. I sold the little houses. I went into an area no one else would go into, and I listed and sold the small houses."

Top listor Carole Kelby (of 200-agent Thorsen Realty), who employs her own full-time secretary to help her with as many as 32 listings at a time, agrees that the listings from the area she farms provide "a *constant* source of income."

Another reason for farming is suggested by the results obtained from a telephone company survey of several cities.

Each year, out of every 100 people:

16–18% move or die.

26–29% change their address, their employment, and so on.

17–19% move into town or come of age.

WHERE?

Most of the real estate salespersons who work a farm agree that it should be made up of the kinds of houses that appeal to the salesperson. They also agree that it should be an area in which the real estate salesperson enjoys working. They suggest that it is helpful if the salesperson lives within the boundaries of the farm.

As far as Don Nourse is concerned, the selection criteria should include the factors of size, age, price, and turnover. A real estate salesperson's farm should not exceed 500 houses, especially if he or she is new in the business. The development should be about three years old. It should not be a new tract, because it takes about 1½ or 2 years before a development starts to turn.

Do not go for high-priced properties, but for turnover. "The key is turnover. Not only because this will make you money, but also because it will make you feel better. Making $1,000 each on five transactions is more fun than closing one deal for $5,000. And it's safer. Losing one out of five is better than risking one fall-through on only one transaction."

According to Dan Bloomquist, a farm should meet the following criteria.

1. It should be in a convenient area. Schools, shopping, churches, parks, bus transportation, and automobile thoroughfares must be reasonably accessible.

2. It should be in a salable area. The overall area must be attractive and on the upgrade, with a lot of amenities.

3. It should be in a transient area. This condition can be met if the houses have a built-in obsolescence factor, so that in two or three years their occupants will outgrow them. It can also be met if the houses are situated near military installations or in communities in which much employment is obtained from national companies whose employees are subject to transfer.

4. It should be in an area whose homes are priced in mid-range. In any given community, there is always a demand for medium-priced homes, regardless of overall economic conditions. What constitutes "mid-range" varies, of course, from one locale to another. A general rule is that the most easily marketable houses are those which do not exceed FHA and VA financing limits. When economic conditions are good, people move out of homes in this price range and into more expensive homes.

5. It should be in an area whose homes are sold by builders. Most builders do not have resale departments within their firms. And those who do rarely make much effort to get the houses back as listings when the houses are resold. Furthermore, the building company salesperson who originally sells a home is a "new home" salesperson who does not handle resales. The owners really do not know a real estate salesperson. It is therefore easier for the "farmer" to become their real estate salesperson.

Homes in older areas, on the other hand, have been individually purchased through the agents of different real estate brokers. Many of these homeowners intend to use the same agents again when they sell. This is especially likely to happen if the real estate salesperson maintains contact with his or her clients.

HOW?

"In two weeks or less," says Nourse, "you can become an expert." Don's remark suggests an ability which becomes glaringly evident when one is surveying the top listors. The edge they have over competitors and nonprofessionals is their ability to know:

1. *What* information they should have.
2. *Where* to get the information.
3. How to *assess* the information.
4. How to *package* the information.
5. How to *utilize* the information to make money.

Later chapters will discuss items 4 and 5. But let us pause now to note some vital sources of information.

Sources of information necessary and helpful to the real estate salesperson may be obtained from private services, trade associations, and the government. These sources include newspapers, magazines, telephone books, MLS, crisscross/reverse directories, tax rolls, and maps.

The importance of R. L. Polk's *City Directory* to the real estate salesperson has been suggested. Another directory with which the real estate salesperson should become acquainted is *Cole's Directory*.

COLE'S DIRECTORY

This large volume was formerly known as *Bressers*. As the publisher states, "It's really seven books in one." In fact, in some areas it is eight books in one.

"The Street Address Directory" (Book 1) shows the names of telephone subscribers at each street address, with zip codes and street locations.

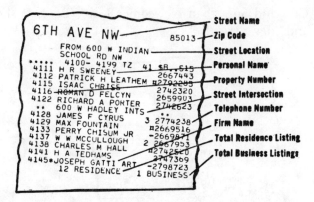

"The Numerical Telephone Directory" (Book 2) shows the name of each telephone subscriber according to the numerical sequence of his or her telephone number.

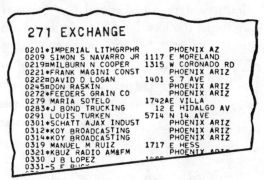

"The Office Building Directory" (Book 3) shows the names, titles, and occupations of tenants in each office building, according to room number.

EQUITABLE LIFE
BUILDING

JACK HADLEY
BUILDING MANAGER   2588411
1802 N CENTRAL

1807 N CENTRAL

ZIP CODE 85004

102 CORONADO COFFEE SH 2526480
108 SHEET METAL PROGRM 2542050
    AIR CNDTN CNTRCTRS 2540175
112 G R TOPE INS   2583421
    ED MIHALEK INS   2583421
    ROBERT P COWIE INS 2583421
    LASHER&ASSOC INS   2583421
    D F LASHER INS   2583421
115 JACK T FULLER ATTY 2538359
2 FLR. EQUTBL LF ASSRNC 2546421
203 J W SWEENEY CPA   2546421
    PAUL ESKEW INS

"The City and Suburban Newcomer List" (Book 4) shows "new listings" and "new arrivals."

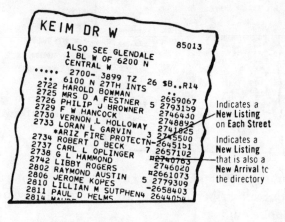

Indicates a New Listing on Each Street

Indicates a New Listing that is also a New Arrival to the directory

"The City, County, State, and Federal Government Officials Directory" (Book 5) shows the locations and telephone numbers of city, county, state, and federal agencies and their key officials.

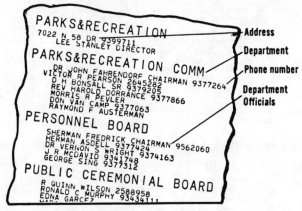

Address

Department

Phone number

Department Officials

The "Census Tract Marketing Section" and "Zip Code Marketing Section" (Book 6) include maps, street guides, counts (a counting of items has been performed and tabulated, e.g., p. 36), and demographic data on each census tract and each zip code covered in the directory (see p. 35, top left).

By looking at the Buying Power maps (or at the "Census Tract Marketing Section"), real estate salespersons can identify which area of the community may be of interest to them. For example, a real estate salesperson may decide to investigate the area bounded by Osborn and Camelback roads between 20th and 28th streets. That area is identified as Trading Zone 45.

Then, by referring to the "Zip Code Marketing Section" marked TZ 45, the salesperson will note the wealth rating for that tract.

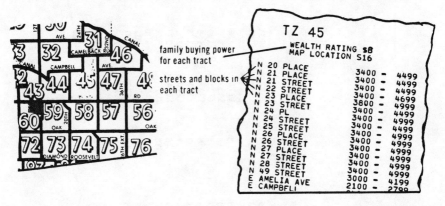

family buying power for each tract

streets and blocks in each tract

TZ 45

WEALTH RATING $B
MAP LOCATION S16

N 20 PLACE	3400 -	4499
N 21 PLACE	3400 -	4499
N 21 STREET	3400 -	4499
N 22 STREET	3400 -	4499
N 23 PLACE	3800 -	4699
N 23 STREET	3800 -	4999
N 24 PL	3400 -	4499
N 24 STREET	3400 -	4999
N 25 STREET	3400 -	4499
N 26 PLACE	3400 -	4999
N 26 STREET	3400 -	4999
N 27 PLACE	3400 -	4999
N 27 STREET	3400 -	4999
N 28 STREET	3400 -	4999
N 49 STREET	3400 -	4999
E AMELIA AVE	3000 -	4199
E CAMPBELL	2100 -	2799

"The Family Income Level and Buying Power Guide" (Book 7) shows the average wealth and income rating on each street.

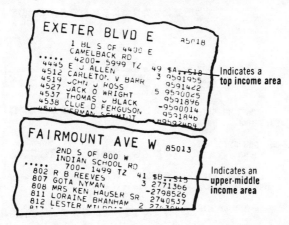

EXETER BLVD E   85018

1 BL S OF 4400 E
CAMELBACK RD
4200- 5999 TZ   49 $A--S18
4445 E J ALLEN   3 9591955
4512 CARLETON V BARR   9591422
4519 JOHN J ROSS   5 9590065
4527 JACK O WRIGHT   9591896
4537 THOMAS J BLACK   -9590014
4538 CLUE D FERGUSON   9591846
4541 HERMAN SCHMIDT   9592404

Indicates a **top income area**

FAIRMOUNT AVE W   85013

2ND S OF 800 W
INDIAN SCHOOL RD
700- 1499 TZ   41 $B--S15
802 R B REEVES   3 2771366
807 GOTA NYMAN   -2798526
808 MRS KEN HAUSER SR   2740537
811 LORAINE BRANHAM   2 271364
812 LESTER MILDD

Indicates an **upper-middle income area**

The prefatory section of the book includes a Housing Unit Analysis, as shown on p. 36.

For some communities, *Cole's Directory* also contains a "Real Estate Section," divided by street, which shows the address of a real estate sale, name of the buyer, the date of purchase, the amount of the sale (indicated by the cost of the revenue stamps or the documentary fee—for example, 370 = $37,000), and the county in which the sale occurred (see p. 37).

TRADING ZONE	MAP LOCATION	WEALTH RATING	MEDIAN AGE *	MEDIAN # PERSONS PER HOUSEHOLD	PERCENT OWNER OCCUPIED HOUSEHOLD	PERCENT FAMILIES WITH CHILDREN UNDER 12	MEDIAN YEARS SCHOOL COMPLETED	HOUSING UNIT ANALYSIS % OF HOUSING UNITS THAT ARE: **			RESIDENTIAL COUNTS		BUSINESS COUNTS (EXCLUDING GOV. & OFFICE BLDGS)	
								1 UNIT STRUCTURE	3 OR MORE UNIT STRUCTURES	10 OR MORE UNIT STRUCTURES	TOTAL	TOTAL NEW	TOTAL	TOTAL NEW
3201	J8	D	45	1.7	8	8	12.7	8	85	56	2622	931	96	25
3202	J8	C	48	1.8	9	5	12.9	12	80	55	1685	583	105	23
3203	J8	A	49	2.7	73	24	14.3	79	8	0	1464	263	188	35
33	J8	B	50	3.0	76	28	13.0	81	8	3	1274	230	144	33
34	J9	C	54	2.6	80	18	12.6	79	13	10	3439	655	259	68
35	J6	E	47	3.2	63	36	9.4	92	3	2	1531	199	686	122
3601	J7	E	47	3.3	45	39	9.9	91	3	0	1362	169	113	16
3602	J7	E	45	3.5	60	41	11.4	94	1	0	1355	176	87	14
3603	J7	D	47	3.2	67	34	12.2	89	4	1	1210	145	74	17
3701	J7	E	50	2.1	23	11	12.6	34	49	28	1134	337	318	96
3702	J8	E	42	2.0	18	12	12.7	25	62	30	2070	784	112	31
3703	J8	D	44	2.1	28	13	12.7	40	47	32	1457	498	66	16
38	J8	D	51	2.2	43	15	12.6	64	23	16	2176	501	816	198
3901	J9	A	57	2.5	85	18	14.4	76	18	17	1659	181	256	56
3902	J9	B	53	2.8	87	19	12.7	92	1	0	1647	227	193	33
4001	J10	B	47	2.6	48	22	13.6	61	32	24	2819	751	332	57
4002	J10	A	50	3.2	93	32	14.9	95	1	0	1253	127	252	34
4003	K10	C	45	3.2	83	42	12.8	89	5	4	2169	539	77	10
4004	K11										792	155	41	5
														0

COLE'S ✕

LEHIGH PL E

8200	J R BECKETT	3	4	70	271	E	DE
8220	C V EDWARDS JR	2	5	73	360		DE
8240	D V HOLCOMBE	4	26	71	270	E	DE
8240	R P FARACI	7	7	71	384		DE

LEHIGH PL W

10617	R L BERGLUND	5	17	73	277		JE
10627	G E HETTINGER	5	17	73	276	E	JE
10628	L D BOLACK	7	11	73	301	E	JE
10638	L J JOHNSON	5	24	73	315	E	JE
	C L HAWKINS	11	6	74	350	E	JE

LEHIGH ST

1010	D O WELCH	11	27	72	359	E	BO
1040	F D GLOVER	5	31	72	360	E	BO
1150	P B HUFF	7	26	72	300	E	BO
1195	N SCLAMBERG	8	27	72	190	E	DE
1240	G E CRAWFORD	6	26	74	323	E	BO
1250	B WEBER	9	19	73	360	E	BO
1340	R TRAVIS	9	25	72	375	E	BO
1420	T A GOLDHAWK JR	6	21	72	315	E	BO
1430	O A VON HAKE	8	20	71	343	E	BO
1450	R D SLOVIKOSKI	4	21	70	275	E	BO
1510	W E TABER	1	27	72	318	E	BO
1540	C E LUGINBILL	6	27	72	289	E	BO
1550	J R HAWLEY	11	18	70	320	E	BO
1570	R WEYDE	10	17	71	405	E	BO
1590	P H BURCHETT	8	11	71	262	E	BO
1650	A P VALDEN	4	17	72	255	E	BO
1710	W E BOCIM	6	27	72	336	E	BO
1760	J L DICK	10	9	74	490	E	BO
1860	E T GRAVES	9	15	72	360	E	BO
1875	R VICKREY	11	24	72	448	E	BO
1890	R J CARLEY	10			33A	F	BO

LEWISTON ST

6086	E B SCHEAFFER JR	9	19	73	373	E	JE
6112	E B STEGEMAN	1	16	74	255	E	JE
6113	E C E GOETZ	6	17	74	310	E	JE
6123	J L VANRELCO INC	2	23	71	273	E	JE
6810	J K C NEWSFIELD	10	25	71	285	E	JE
	D V CAMBLIN	1		72	317	E	JE
7610	A R ROSS	1	25	72	345	E	JE
7611	F H RIEDEL	3	26	72	350	E	JE
7641	J J YOUNGGREEN	6	28	73	399	E	JE
7670	D D LANE	1	30	74	375	E	JE
7710	F F URBANEK JR	1	30	72	690	E	JE
7710	D F DRAKE	1	30	72	415	E	JE
7740	C L KNITTLE	11	30	72	490	E	JE
7780	J U BELK	5	17	73	401	E	JE
7830	R J EVERITT	5	20	72	359	E	JE
7850	R J BEANGLE	8	27	73	361	E	JE
7851	R J BEALS	4	23	73	348	E	JE
7870	J MITCHELL	12	19	73	500	E	JE
7871	N B ENGEL	2	10	73	535	E	JE
7890	D V PHYE JR	2	9	72	630	E	JE
7891	D I PICCONE	8	21	72	405	E	JE
7910	H G REBLE	5	13	72	272	E	JE
7911	R K MODGLIN JR	8	7	73	339	E	JE
	OLSON			72	348	E	JE
	HELD				358	E	J

LEWIS CT'S

1875	E M DUNSTAN	1	11	73	54	E	JE
2550	E R FUSS	8	17	74	355	E	JE
2595	J WILDER	3	22	73	389	E	JE
3716	D F GREEN	8	31	72	245	E	JE
3726	G K DAVISON	7	13	72	237	E	JE
3727	X A PROMUTICO	7	16	72	339	E	JE
3733	O J RATHMAN JR	3	14	72	267	E	JE
3735	A W RENSHAW	1	25	73	239	E	JE
4525	R VAN DE WERKEN	6	27	72	360	E	JE
4534	J NELSON	10	30	74	318	E	JE
4535	I R MCCART	10	18	71	316	E	JE
4715	O R VREDENBURGH	10	28	71	306	E	JE
4725	F R WOLFE	10	16	71	304	E	JE
	RINO	5	27	71	284	E	J

LEHIGH AVE

1111	E A SMITH	10	23	74	311	E	LO
1118	A CARMICHAEL	9	16	74	303	E	LO
1123	E G FORTIER	9	7	71	308	E	LO
1124	J J BOWSER	9	17	74	314	E	LO
1129	A T KNOCH	6	24	71	290	E	LO
1131	H C TUMBLIN	17	12	72	343	E	LO
1135	J K FOX	12	12	74	304	E	LO
1136	A T GRIDER III	10	23	72	321	E	LO
1141	D J HIGGINS III	10	6	74	294	E	JO
1142	R D KYLE	11	14	73	323	E	LO
1148	J J HARVEY	17	7	73	275	E	JO
1154	A C WALKER JR	10	17	73	319	E	LO
1159	M C MCGIRR	19		73	317	E	LO
1160	F L MALOWICK	10	17	73	332	E	LO
1171	J D FREDEN	10	29	74	328	E	LO
1206	I R SCHNEIDER	3	3	74	296	E	LO
1207	J J KELLY	10	3	74	289	E	LO
1217	J C TRUMBLE	10	24	74	331	E	LO
1218	G R GREULING	30		72	321	E	LO
1218	J O A PERRNER	3	9		310	E	LO

LEHIGH AVE

1250	G B PEET JR	9	23	70	239	E	BO
1350	J B GREINER	8	3	71	266	E	BO
1550	G I MAYES	9	7	72	320	E	JE
10161	E J ORTEGA				236	E	JE

LEHIGH AVE E

5559	J H RHODES	4	10	72	439	E	DE
5560	G F RASKIN	2	12	71	480	E	DE
5570	J F KUSKULIS	4	20	71	550	E	DE
8005	H A COLLINS			71	340	E	DE
8086	R O MCCLANAHAN	11	3	71	390	E	DE
8196	R R MULHAUSER	11		71	293	E	DE
8246	D D SADOWSKI	6	25	71	311	E	DE
8405	U BERG	10	18	71	360	E	DE
8446	E A WALDROOP	10	16	71	343	E	DE
	CROCCO	10	11	71	390	E	DE

COUNTY ASSISTANCE

Among the 3,000-odd counties with the United States, real estate record-keeping systems vary from county to county. Five major county departments, however, usually provide the data described below.

The Engineering Department

The county engineering department keeps both Mylars and blue-line prints of right-of-way road maps which show sewer lines, water mains, fire hydrants, utility lines, easements, and road dedications. For purposes of new road construction or the improvement of existing roads, such departments need to know what is underneath road rights-of-way as well as what is on the road surface.

These right-of-way road maps are an excellent source for a builder or a developer, and they are always available for public inspection. They can be used as a selling tool, especially in selling unimproved property.

The Planning Department

The county (or area) planning department's master use plan shows zoning patterns, patterns of development, and proposed highway construction for the entire county. Projected population by area, as well as proposals for rapid transit systems, airports, and other major governmental developments, are generally superimposed on master use plans.

The master use plan is a worthwhile working tool for showing the amounts and types of growth that are expected in various neighborhoods.

The Building and Zoning Department

This county department will usually make the county zoning maps available for inspection. Although zoning is often a function of municipalities, county zoning maps are an excellent source of information on zoning by parcel. They also give, usually on a section basis, information on the zoning of bordering parcels.

Such maps can be used not only as a sales tool, but also as an indication of whether a particular parcel can be made to fit in with planned neighborhood growth.

The Clerk's Office

The county clerk's responsiblities include the recording of information which is of major interest to the real estate industry. The county clerk also maintains for open inspection by the public all documents, regardless of age, recorded within the county's jurisdiction. More than 200 different types of documents may be recorded, but deeds and mortgages account for almost 30 percent of such documents. When compiled geographically, deeds and mortgages form the nucleus of comparable sales information.

Other real estate documents which are recorded in considerable volume by the county clerk include notices of commencement, liens, tax liens, foreclosures, assignments of mortgage, satisfactions of mortgage, and land contracts.

Any document going into the official record book of the county clerk is scanned to make sure that it has all the elements needed.

The taxes are calculated and collected by a cashier, and stamps and certification are affixed to the document. The document is then filmed, and the original is returned to the proper party. The filmed copy then becomes the official public record. It is numbered and cataloged in a fashion that makes it accessible to the public.

Other public record files which are often maintained under the recorder's jurisdiction include copies of recorded plat maps and declarations of condominium plans. These sources can be used in determining the layouts of lots and of condominium projects.

The recorder is required by law to have *direct, indirect, legal,* and *file number* indexes available to the public.

The *direct* index is an alphabetical list of all first parties on each instrument. The *indirect* index is an alphabetical list of all second parties on each instrument.

The *legal* description index is normally broken down into a section/township/range index for unplatted properties and a plat book and page index, or a subname index, for platted properties.

The recorder's *file number* index is a numerical-chronological listing of each instrument as it is recorded. The index generally shows the type of instrument, the date and time it was recorded, and the makers of the instrument. The recorder maintains his inventory system on a chronological basis because this is the only practical way to handle the heavy day-to-day volume. Since the recorder's file number index is kept chronologically rather than geographically, the recorder's legal index is required in order to make practical real estate applications of the file number index.

The county clerk's office is required to supply a copy of each individual deed to the county property assessor's office. This document is then used by the assessor to update his inventory of parcel ownership. The form of the deed varies from county to county, but it must include the names of the grantee and the grantor, the date, the record book and page, the legal description of the property, document stamps, and the address of the grantee.

The Property Assessor's Office

The county property assessor must enumerate every parcel of real property within the county and determine its market value. This is normally accomplished with two types of files:

1. A map file which shows the physical property lines of each parcel of real estate.
2. A tax roll file which shows the name of the taxpayer, his or her address and some identifying number (which relates to the map volume), the land value, the improvement value, and the exemptions to which the owner is entitled.

The assessor's records and value findings are later used by the tax collector's office (which in most cases is a different department with a different purpose).

Once the county commission has adopted the county budget for a given year, it is the property assessor's function to distribute this amount equitably over all the properties in the county on the basis of the market value appraisal. This budget and the valuation of the county property together create the tax *rate*.

All of the county assessor's records (except for his working documents) are considered public information and must be maintained in such a way as to be easily accessible to the public. The assessor, however, is *not* required to index his records in the same way that the county clerk is required to file his. The assessor's number system is strictly for his own use in keeping track of his inventory. These documents generally include the tax maps, the tax roll, and the mass appraisal file, usually referred to as property record cards.

Property record cards are normally individual record cards for each parcel, diagramming the layout of the structure on a piece of property, and enumerating its major construction characteristics, the year it was constructed, and its size.

These documents are, of course, invaluable aids to the real estate industry.

The county property assessor uses a geographic "strap" numbering system. (*Strap* stands for section-township-range-area-parcel number.) This system relates back to the section-township-range survey, and picks up the developer's numbers from a plat to complete the number. This system greatly eases the problem of going from the legal description of a property to the tax numbering system.

The tax map numbering system is broken down in this manner:

Assessor's Number

01	30	14	42030	049	0040
↓	↓	↓	↓	↓	↓
A	B	C	D	E	F

A. The first two digits indicate the section number.

B. The next two digits indicate the township number.

C. The next two digits indicate the range number.

D. The following five digits are the subdivision number (which would be zeroes in the case of unplatted property).

E. The next three digits indicate the subdivision block number (or the parcel number in the case of acreage).

F. The final four digits indicate the subdivision lot number, the last position being reserved for lot split identification (in the case of unsubdivided property, the last four digits are for acreage and parcel splits).

This numbering system simplifies finding a parcel in the tax roll, since the tax roll is sequenced the same way that the developer sequenced his lot and block numbers.

The different county departments, then, usually work together in the following manner: The county clerk, through the recording department, provides the county property assessor with updates (in the form of deeds) for the tax roll file. The file then developed by the

FIGURE 4-1
REDI Service Areas

ALABAMA
COUNTY/AREA	MAJOR CITY
Jefferson	Birmingham
Madison	Huntsville
Montgomery	Montgomery

ARIZONA
COUNTY/AREA	MAJOR CITY
†* Maricopa	Phoenix
†* Pima	Tucson
Pinal	Casa Grande

ARKANSAS
COUNTY/AREA	MAJOR CITY
Pulaski	Little Rock

CALIFORNIA
COUNTY/AREA	MAJOR CITY
†* Alameda	Oakland
†* Contra Costa	Concord/Richmond
Fresno	Fresno
Humboldt	Eureka
Kern	Bakersfield
†* Los Angeles	Los Angeles
†* Marin	San Rafael
Mendocino	Ukiah
Merced	Merced
Monterey	Salinas
Napa	Napa
† Orange	Anaheim
Riverside	Riverside
Sacramento	Sacramento
†* San Bernardino	San Bernardino
†* San Diego	San Diego
†* San Francisco	San Francisco
San Joaquin	Stockton
San Luis Obispo	San Luis Obispo
†* San Mateo	San Mateo
Santa Barbara	Santa Barbara
†* Santa Clara	San Jose
†* Santa Cruz	Santa Cruz
Shasta	Redding
†* Solano	Vallejo
†* Sonoma	Santa Rosa
Stanislaus	Modesto
Tulare	Visalia
†* Ventura	Oxnard

COLORADO
COUNTY/AREA	MAJOR CITY
†* Adams	Aurora
†* Arapahoe	Englewood
Denver	Denver
Douglas	Castle Rock
El Paso	Colorado Springs
†* Jefferson	Lakewood

CONNECTICUT
COUNTY/AREA	MAJOR CITY
* Fairfield	Bridgeport

GEORGIA
COUNTY/AREA	MAJOR CITY
Chatham	Savannah
* Clayton	Forest Park
* Cobb	Marietta
Coweta	Newnan
De Kalb	Atlanta
Fayette	Fayetteville
Forsyth	Cumming
* Fulton	Atlanta
* Gwinnett	Lawrenceville
Henry	Mc Donough
Newton	Covington
Paulding	Dallas

HAWAII
COUNTY/AREA	MAJOR CITY
* Hawaii	Hilo
* Honolulu	Honolulu
* Kalawao	Kuhului
* Kauai	Kappa
Maui	Kahului

ILLINOIS
COUNTY/AREA	MAJOR CITY
† Cook	Chicago
La Salle	Ottawa
Will	Joliet

INDIANA
COUNTY/AREA	MAJOR CITY
Clark	Jeffersonville
Floyd	New Albany
* Marion	Indianapolis

KANSAS
COUNTY/AREA	MAJOR CITY
Sedgwick	Wichita

KENTUCKY
COUNTY/AREA	MAJOR CITY
Fayette	Lexington
†* Jefferson	Louisville

LOUISIANA
COUNTY/AREA	MAJOR CITY
* Orleans	New Orleans

MARYLAND
COUNTY/AREA	MAJOR CITY
* Anne Arundel	Annapolis
* Baltimore	Baltimore
Frederick	Frederick
Howard	Columbia
* Montgomery	Silver Springs
Prince Georges	Bowie

NEW YORK
COUNTY/AREA	MAJOR CITY
* Monroe	Rochester
Nassau	Levittown
Orange	Newburgh
Putnam	Mahopac
Queens	Jamaica, NYC
* Rockland	New City
* Suffolk	Brentwood
* Westchester	Yonkers

NORTH CAROLINA
COUNTY/AREA	MAJOR CITY
Buncombe	Asheville
Forsyth	Winston-Salem
* Guilford	Greensboro
* Mecklenburg	Charlotte
* Wake	Raleigh

OHIO
COUNTY/AREA	MAJOR CITY
Butler	Hamilton
Clark	Springfield
†* Cuyahoga	Cleveland
* Franklin	Columbus
Geauga	Chardon
Greene	Fairborn
* Hamilton	Cincinnati
Lake	Mentor
* Montgomery	Dayton

OREGON
COUNTY/AREA	MAJOR CITY
Clackamas	Milwaukie
Multnomah	Portland
Lane	Eugene
Washington	Beaverton

PENNSYLVANIA
COUNTY/AREA	MAJOR CITY
Beaver	Aliquippa
†* Bucks	Levittown
†* Chester	West Chester
Cumberland	Camp Hill
Dauphin	Harrisburg
Erie	Erie
Lancaster	Lancaster
Lehigh	Allentown
Monroe	East Stroudsburg
* Montgomery	Norristown
Northampton	Bethlehem
York	York

SOUTH CAROLINA
COUNTY/AREA	MAJOR CITY
* Charleston	Charleston
Florence	Florence
†* Greenville	Greenville
* Richland	Columbia
* Spartanburg	Spartanburg

DELAWARE
* New Castle · · · Wilmington

FLORIDA
* Alachua · · · Gainesville
* Bay · · · Panama City
†* Brevard · · · Melbourne
†* Broward · · · Ft. Lauderdale
* Charlotte · · · Port Charlotte
Citrus · · · Inverness
Clay · · · Orange Park
* Collier · · · Naples
Columbia · · · Lake City
†* Dade · · · Miami
De Soto · · · Arcadia
Duval · · · Jacksonville
* Escambia · · · Pensacola
Flagler · · · Bunnell
Hardee · · · Wauchula
Hernando · · · Brooksville
†* Hillsborough · · · Tampa
†* Indian River · · · Vero Beach
* Lake · · · Leesburg
†* Lee · · · Fort Myers
* Leon · · · Tallahassee
Levy · · · Chiefland
* Manatee · · · Bradenton
* Marion · · · Ocala
* Martin · · · Stuart
†* Monroe · · · Key West
Nassau · · · Fernandina Beach
* Okaloosa · · · Ft. Walton Beach
†* Orange · · · Orlando
* Osceola · · · Kissimmee
†* Palm Beach · · · West Palm Beach
†* Pasco · · · Newport Richey
†* Pinellas · · · St. Petersburg
* Polk · · · Lakeland
Putnam · · · Palatka
St. Johns · · · St. Augustine
†* St. Lucie · · · Ft. Pierce
Santa Rosa · · · Milton
†* Sarasota · · · Sarasota
†* Seminole · · · Sanford
Sumter · · · Wildwood
Suwannee · · · Live Oak
* Volusia · · · Daytona Beach, De Land
Walton · · · De Funiak Springs

MASSACHUSETTS
* Cape Cod Area · · · Hyannis

MICHIGAN
* Macomb · · · Warren
* Oakland · · · Royal Oak
Washtenaw · · · Ann Arbor

MISSISSIPPI
City of Jackson · · · Jackson

MISSOURI
Jackson · · · Kansas City
* St. Louis · · · Florissant

NEVADA
* Clark · · · Las Vegas
Washoe · · · Reno

NEW MEXICO
Bernalillo · · · Albuquerque

NEW JERSEY
* Atlantic · · · Atlantic City
* Bergen · · · Teaneck
†* Burlington · · · Willingboro
†* Camden · · · Camden
Cape May · · · Ocean City
Cumberland · · · Vineland
Essex · · · Newark
†* Gloucester · · · Glassboro
* Hudson · · · Jersey City
* Hunterdon · · · Lumbertville
* Mercer · · · Trenton
* Middlesex · · · Edison
†* Monmouth · · · Long Branch
†* Morris · · · Morristown
†* Ocean · · · Lakewood
†* Passaic · · · Paterson
* Salem · · · Pennsville
†* Somerset · · · North Plainfield
† Sussex · · · Hopatcong
* Union · · · Elizabeth
* Warren · · · Phillipsburg

NEW YORK
Broome · · · Binghamton
Erie · · · Buffalo
Kings · · · Brooklyn, NYC
Manhattan · · · Manhattan

TENNESSEE
†* Davidson · · · Nashville
• Hamilton · · · Chattanooga
Knox · · · Knoxville
• Shelby · · · Memphis

TEXAS
Bexar · · · San Antonio
Collin · · · Plano
• Dallas · · · Dallas
Denton · · · Denton
El Paso · · · El Paso
* Tarrant · · · Fort Worth

UTAH
Davis · · · Bountiful
Salt Lake · · · Salt Lake City
Utah · · · Provo
Weber · · · Ogden

VIRGIN ISLANDS
St. Croix · · · Christiansted
St. John · · · Cruz Bay
St. Thomas · · · Charlotte Amalie

VIRGINIA
* Arlington · · · Arlington
* Chesterfield · · · Bon Air
City of Alexandria · · · Alexandria
City of Hampton · · · Hampton
City of Newport News · · · Newport News
City of Norfolk · · · Norfolk
* City of Richmond · · · Richmond
* Fairfax · · · Annandale
Fauquier · · · Warrenton
Loudoun · · · Sterling
* Prince William · · · Woodbridge
Roanoke · · · Roanoke
Spotsylvania · · · Spotsylvania
Stafford · · · Ferry Farms
York · · · Poquoson

WASHINGTON
King · · · Seattle
Pierce · · · Tacoma
Spokane · · · Spokane

WISCONSIN
* Milwaukee · · · Milwaukee
* Waukesha · · · Waukesha

* . . . AERIAL/MAP COVERAGE AVAILABLE IN THESE COUNTIES.
† . . . REALTY SALES SERVICE AVAILABLE IN THESE COUNTIES.

property appraisal office is generally passed on to the county tax collector, who calculates the exemptions, computes the tax bills and sends them to the owners.

The mapping function performed in the property assessor's office often will be shared with the building and zoning departments. For example, by adding zoning to the property assessor's maps, the assessor's maps become zoning maps.

REDI

One of the best sources of real estate information is a company known as REDI. Real Estate Data, Inc. (2398 N.W. 119th Street, Miami, Florida), is the nation's largest supplier of real estate maps and ownership information. This rapidly expanding company serves as an information resource for over 100,000 real estate professionals in hundreds of cities and counties in 35 states and the Virgin Islands (see Figure 4–1).

REDI reproduces real estate information on file in county offices. This material is then leased to such subscribers as brokers, appraisers, mortgage bankers, title insurance companies, savings and loan associations, public utilities, surveyors, and government agencies. The volumes of compiled and reproduced data are donated to the county offices from which the data are obtained. Should you or your broker not subscribe to the service, you may find the books in the county assessor's office.

The extent, depth, and variety of the information and services provided by REDI locally depend upon the sophistication demanded by the real estate activities in a given county.

Aerial Photographs

For years, aerial photographs have been invaluable to commercial and industrial specialists, land developers, and the like (see Figure 4–2). But since these photographs were usually custom-made, their cost prohibited their use by most residential brokers. Not only did relatively few brokers use them, but many sales associates did not even know they existed.

During the past few years, however, REDI has made inexpensive aerial photographs available to residential brokerage offices. Real estate salespeople are now able to use them daily as graphic sales aids.

FIGURE 4–2
A Partial Aerial Photograph

1. UNION ST
2. MONCLAIR RD
5. HIGHLAND AVE

The residential real estate saleperson can use aerial photographs as follows:

1. Since aerials give a much more comprehensive view of a market area than is obtainable from ground level, an aerial photograph can give prospects their "first look" at a specific piece of property. Aerials provide a contrasting perspective to the one prospects will get on the property itself. Or, to reverse the procedure, aerials can show prospects where they have been.

2. Aerials show travel routes and neighborhood selling points, such as recreational facilities (parks, golf courses, tennis courts), schools, churches, shopping centers, and freeways. Aerials also show distances in relation to a specific property.

3. Aerials show area-by-area growth trends (for example, new subdivisions). On the other hand, they can also demonstrate the absence of growth possibilities in settled areas. A collection of aerials from year to year will show the growth or stability of an area. Such photos can be made into office murals for use in plotting current listings, sales, and the like.

4. Aerials can be mailed to out-of-town clients who are unfamiliar with an area.

5. Aerials can be used in market analyses.

6. Aerials are ideal for compiling farm presentation packages.

7. After the closing, aerials can be presented to clients as a thank-you gesture.

One real estate salesperson successfully convinced FSBOs to list with him by marking on an aerial photograph all the competing homes for sale in the FSBO's area.

Property Identification Maps

Property identification maps are equally valuable to the real estate salesperson (see Figure 4–3).

1. Property maps display the configuration of a particular parcel and its size as compared to that of surrounding parcels. A property map may be used as a prelude to using an aerial in "first looking" at a property (or vice versa).

2. Property maps show the environmental "mix" in a given area and the area's projected developmental future.

3. Property maps aid the listing process by reflecting lot dimen-

FIGURE 4–3
Sample (partial) Land Section Map

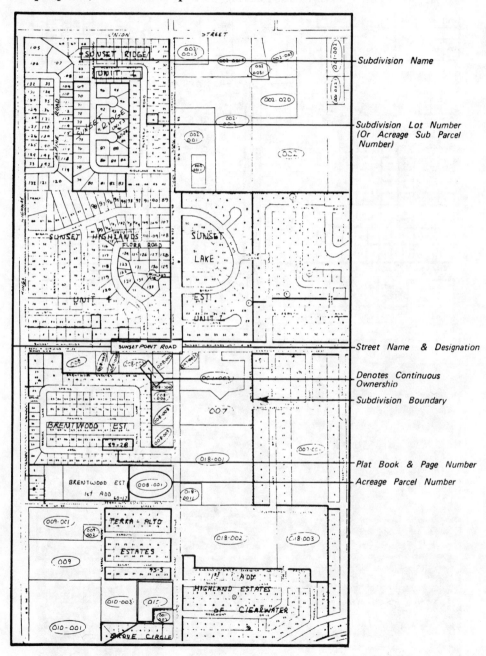

— Subdivision Name

— Subdivision Lot Number
(Or Acreage Sub Parcel
Number)

— Street Name & Designation

— Denotes Continuous
Ownership

— Subdivision Boundary

— Plat Book & Page Number

— Acreage Parcel Number

48

FIGURE 4–4
Sample (partial) Aerial Photograph and Matching Maps

sions, since it is not uncommon for owners to be in error about the size of their property.

4. Since property maps are easily and inexpensively reproduced, they may, like aerials, be presented to out-of-town prospects, used in farm presentations, and so on.

5. Since property maps are made to the same scale as aerial photographs, they can be cross-referenced to aerials (see Figure 4–4).

6. The real estate salesperson can attach his or her business card to a photocopied property map and present the map (1) to prospects as a reminder of property he or she showed them (and as a reminder of who showed it to them); (2) to clients, along with their house papers, as a reminder of who sold the property to them when the time comes to list the real estate again and; (3) to FSBOs as a reminder of who *should* be selling their property for them.

Ownership Rolls

Ownership rolls (also known as tax rolls or assessment rolls) are the most important single compendium of information available to the real estate agent (see Figures 4–5 and 4–6).

1. Since the ownership roll is a complete and accurate geographic inventory of every parcel of property in a county, it includes vital details on every piece of real estate. The roll can be used to identify and reach the owner (whether local or out-of-town). In cases of trust or corporate ownership, it identifies the true owner.

2. The ownership roll aids in generating listings by facilitating *selective* mailing programs (*by property price* based on assessed values or *by area* in a specific subdivision) and *saturation* mailing programs (in areas where activity is high).

3. The ownership roll may be used to preplan telephone and house-to-house canvassing, since it preidentifies owners by name (among other facts), thereby improving the first contact with the prospect.

4. Since the ownership roll legally describes every property in a county, it may be used to prepare listing agreements, to verify a legal description, and to identify owners of multiple lots within the same parcel.

5. The ownership roll includes a "land use" (or property classification) code that describes every parcel by its present use: single

FIGURE 4–5
Sample Ownership (Tax Roll) Information

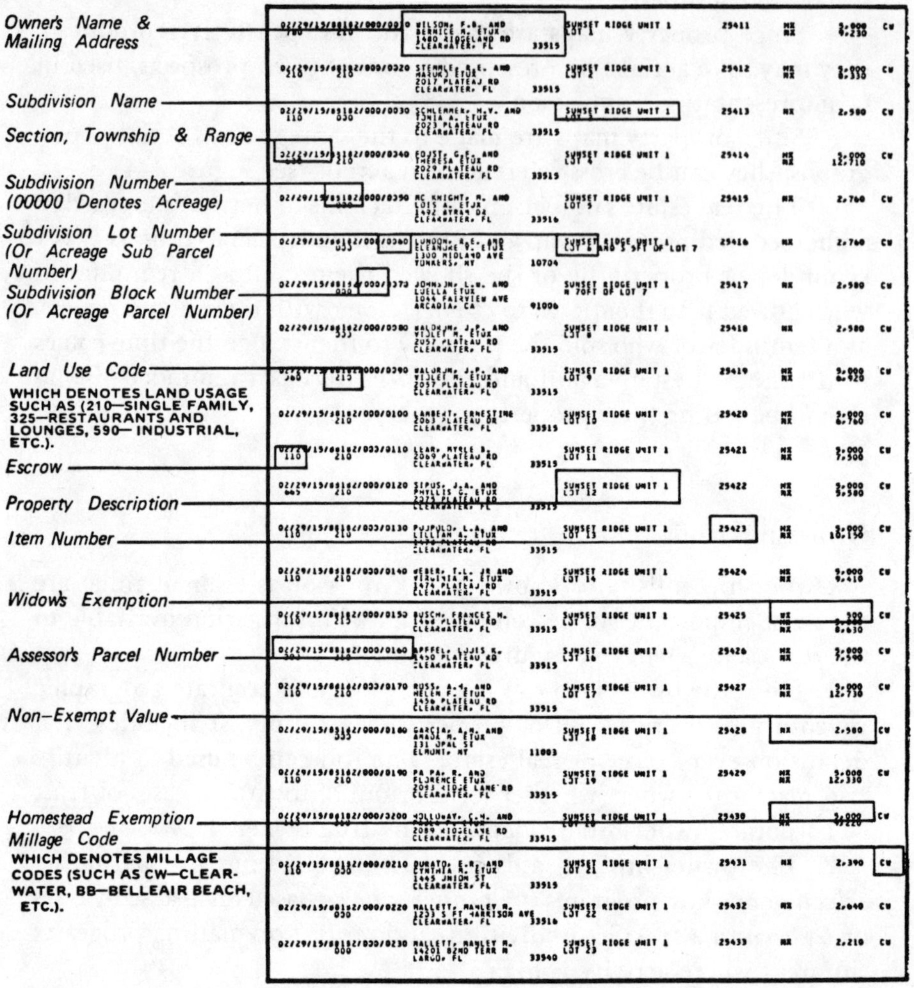

Owner's Name & Mailing Address

Subdivision Name

Section, Township & Range

Subdivision Number
(00000 Denotes Acreage)

Subdivision Lot Number
(Or Acreage Sub Parcel Number)

Subdivision Block Number
(Or Acreage Parcel Number)

Land Use Code
WHICH DENOTES LAND USAGE SUCH AS (210—SINGLE FAMILY, 325—RESTAURANTS AND LOUNGES, 590— INDUSTRIAL, ETC.).

Escrow

Property Description

Item Number

Widow's Exemption

Assessor's Parcel Number

Non-Exempt Value

Homestead Exemption
Millage Code
WHICH DENOTES MILLAGE CODES (SUCH AS CW—CLEAR-WATER, BB—BELLEAIR BEACH, ETC.).

family, industrial, commercial, vacant land, and the like (see Figure 4–7). Thus it can be used to identify all like properties if there is a prospect with special needs or interests.

6. Since the ownership roll reflects the assessed value of each property, it can be used to find unimproved properties (vacant lots). Furthermore, it is an indicator of relative market value within a given

FIGURE 4-6
Examples of Indexing to Ownership Information

A. Sample section township, and range index

Township Number — [30] ---- 14 --- 1 ------ 35
                                      12 ------ 68
                                      13 ------ 102
Range Number — 27 ----- [15] --- 1 ------ 124
Section Number —   [2] ----- 149
                                   3 ----- 162
Atlas Page Number —   10 ----- [180]
                                  11 ----- 213

B. Sample subdivision index
(listed alphabetically by subdivision name)

Subdivision Name				
IMPERIAL POINT UNIT 3	19-30-15	6R	063--087	3571
INDIAN BEACH REVISED	1-30-14	1R	5-- 6	2
INDIAN BEACH RE-REVISED 1ST ADD	1-30-14	3R	23-- 11	19
INDIAN BEACH RE-REVISED 1ST ADD	1-30-14	3R	23-- 13	19
INDIAN BEACH RE-REVISED 2ND ADD	1-30-14	46	23-- 72	3196
INDIAN BEACH RE-REVISED 2ND ADD	7-30-15	46	23-- 72	3196
INDIAN BEACH RE-REVISED 3RD ADD	1-30-14	47	25-- 30	29
INDIAN BEACH RE-REVISED 3RD ADD	17-30-15	47	25-- 30	29
INDIAN BEACH RE-REVISED 4TH ADD	6-30-15	50	27-- 1	32
INDIAN BEACH RE-REVISED 5TH ADD	6-30-15	51	28-- 77	34
INDIAN BEACH RE-REVISED 6TH ADD	6-30-15	51	27-- 20	35
INDIAN BEACH RE-REVISED 7TH ADD	6-30-15	51	28-- 38	37
INDIAN BEACH RE-REVISED 8TH ADD	6-30-15	52	28-- 89	38

Subdivision Name
Section, Township & Range
Year Recorded
Plat Book & Page Number
Atlas Page Number

FIGURE 4-7
Land Use Codes

000	Vacant land	320	Single-building store (one operation in one store) hardware, tavern, etc.
110	Citrus		
120	Pasture	321	Row stores—two or more units (taverns and apartments)
190	Other		
210	Single family	322	Convenience stores (7–11, Pic Quick, Lil General, Farm Stores, etc.)
220	Duplex–triplex		
221	Town house	323	Chain stores (free-standing super-markets, A&P, etc.)
230	Condominiums		
231	Condominiums–leasehold	324	Shopping centers, department stores, large commercial centers—Grandway, Zayre, etc.
250	Co-op apartments		
260	Mobile homes—lot owned		
290	Other (garages, PC, sheds, etc.) barns, kennels, C.G. shops	325	Restaurants and Lounges—ABC liquor
311	Apartments (four units or more)	326	Restaurants—drive-ins, diners
312	Hotels and motels	327	Ground-floor stores with offices or apartments above
313	Hotels and motels combined with other commercials	329	Other retail (building supplies, nurseries, fruit stands, plumbing and lumber)
314	Mobile home parks (rentals)		
319	Other residential (cottage courts, mixed) more than one house		

FIGURE 4–7 (*continued*)

330	General office (real estate, insurance, etc.
331	Financial (banks, savings and loans)
332	Multistory office buildings (300)
333	Medical offices, clinics
334	Nursing homes, rest homes, private hospitals
335	Funeral homes, mortuaries
336	Post office—nonexempt
339	Other offices (car rentals, etc.), used car lots
340	Bulk plants
341	Service stations
342	Auto dealers (full agencies—Grant's, Ross, etc.)
343	Garages—general repair
344	Auto service centers (Firestone, Goodyear, Midas shops, etc.)
345	Car wash
346	Car storage (trailers, parking lots)
347	Terminals (bus, air, etc.)
348	Marinas (boat sales, storage, etc.)
349	Other transportation (car rental, car junk, car auctions)
350	Bowling lanes, skating rinks
351	Theaters (including drive-ins)
352	Golf courses
353	Clubs—nonexempt
354	Special attractions (aquatariums, wax museums)
359	Other amusements or recreation (dog tracks, car tracks, commercial pools, condo recreation area)
360	Power companies
361	Telephone companies
362	Railroad—comptroller assessed
363	Railroad—tax assessor assessed
364	Water and sewer plants

365	Radio and television stations
369	Other utilities
490	Other commercials, private schools, junk yards
510	Large manufacturers (assessed over $40,000)
520	Small manufacturers (assessed under $40,000), printers
530	Processing plants, (dairy, citrus, bottling, ice, fish, laundry, cleaning and bakeries
540	Public bonded warehouse (rental type), van lines, etc.
541	Commercial storage (Maas Brothers, associated with retailer)
542	Industrial storage (warehouse in conjunction with manufacturing plant)
590	Other industrial
910	Federal
911	State
912	County
913	City
917	County, sanitary district
920	Educational, public
921	Educational, religious
922	Educational, private
930	Churches (Salvation Army)
940	Literary or scientific
950	Charitable/fraternal, civic, Masonic, American Legion, Elks, Lions, K of C, vol. fire department
960	Hospitals
990	Other exempt—Red Cross, Veteran's Law 702, unions, YWCA, YMCA, SPCA, cemetery reservation, and apartments
995	Veterans

area. The roll may also be employed in combination with land use information to pinpoint special types of properties that meet prescribed dollar criteria (for example, all duplexes valued at over $60,000).

7. The ownership roll includes a tax assessment millage code breakdown through which one can determine the exact amount of taxes on any parcel of property in a county as well as additional information, such as the school, election, and fire district in which the property is located (see Figure 4–8).

FIGURE 4–8
Sample Millage Rates (dollars per thousand levied for 1975 taxes in Pinellas County, Florida)

Millage Code	City or District	City or District Millage	County Millage	Fire District Millage	Total School County City or District Millage	City Home-stead Exempt Millage
	County	0.000	7.707	0.000	15.707	0.00
TD	County W I Transit District	0.000	7.707	0.000	15.947 TD	0.00
BB	Belleair Beach	3.000	6.352	0.000	17.352	0.00
BBL	Belleair Bluffs	3.000	6.352	0.000	17.592 TD	0.00
BTF	Belleair Bluffs FID TR	0.000	7.707	1.000	16.947 TD	0.00
BL	Belleair	6.670	6.352	0.000	21.262 TD	0.00
BLO	Belleair (Outside)......	5.780	6.352	0.000	20.372 TD	0.00
BS	Belleair Shore........	3.000	6.352	0.000	17.352	0.00
BVLD	Baywood Village, LT...	0.370	7.707	0.000	16.317 TD	0.00
CCLD	Center City Colony LT	1.040	7.707	0.000	16.987 TD	0.00
CCTF	Clearwater FID Curlew LT, TR	0.890	7.707	3.200	20.037 TD	0.00
CTF	Clearwater FID, TR....	0.000	7.707	3.200	19.147 TD	0.00
CVTF	Clearwater, Virginia LT, FID, TR	1.270	7.707	3.200	20.417 TD	0.00
CW	Clearwater	5.456	6.352	0.000	20.048 TD	0.00
CWD	Clearwater Downtown Dev. Bd.	6.456	6.352	0.000	21.048 TD	0.00
DLTF	Dunedin, Lofty LT, FID, TR	1.370	7.707	3.150	20.467 TD	0.00
DN	Dunedin	5.620	6.352	0.000	20.212 TD	0.00
DTP	Dunedin, FID, TR	0.000	7.707	3.150	19.097 TD	0.00
GF	Gandy, FID, TR	0.000	7.707	2.880	18.827 TD	0.00
GP	Gulfport	3.340	6.352	0.000	17.692	0.00
GPLD	Golden Palm LT, TR..	1.230	7.707	0.000	17.177 TD	0.00
HLTD	Holiday LT, TR	0.450	7.707	0.000	16.397 TD	0.00
HR	Safety Harbor	6.860	6.352	0.000	21.452 TD	0.00
HTF	Safety Harbor, FID TR	0.000	7.707	4.640	20.587 TD	0.00
IPLD	Imperial Point LT	0.430	7.707	0.000	16.377 TD	0.00
IRB	Indian Rocks Bch	3.000	6.352	0.000	17.592 TD	0.00
IS	Indian Shores	3.000	6.352	0.000	17.592 TD	0.00
KC	Kenneth City	3.000	6.352	0.000	17.352	0.00
LA	Largo	1.509	6.352	0.000	16.101 TD	0.00
LNTF	Largo, Newport LT, FID, TR	0.480	7.707	3.240	19.667 TD	0.00
LTF	Largo, FID, TR		7.707	3.240	19.187 TD	0.00
MB	Madeira Beach	4.040	6.352	0.000	18.392	0.00
NRB	N. Redington Bch	4.500	6.352	0.000	19.092 TD	0.00
OM	Oldsmar	4.550	6.352	0.000	19.142 TD	0.00
PF	Pinellas Park FID	0.000	7.707	3.400	19.347 TD	0.00
PP	Pinellas Park	4.580	6.352	0.000	19.172 TD	0.00
RB	Redington Beach	4.250	6.352	0.000	18.842 TD	0.00

FIGURE 4–8 (*continued*)

Millage Code	City or District	City or District Millage	County Millage	Fire District Millage	Total School County City or District Millage	City Home-stead Exempt Millage
RS	Redington Shores	3.000	6.352	0.000	17.592 TD	0.00
RMLD	Ridgewood Mt. Village LT	0.950	7.707	0.000	16.897 TD	0.00
SPA	South Pasadena	1.400	6.352	0.000	15.752	0.00
SPB	St. Petersburg Beach ...	4.500	6.352	0.000	18.852	0.00
SPBS	St. Pete Beach and Sewer District	6.410	6.352	0.000	20.762	0.00
SA	St. Petersburg (1 Ext.)..	7.330	6.352	0.000	21.682	0.33
SB	St. Petersburg (2 Ext.)..	7.150	6.352	0.000	21.502	0.15
SC	St. Petersburg (3 Ext.)..	7.100	6.352	0.000	21.452	0.10
SD	St. Petersburg (no TX bonds)	7.000	6.352	0.000	21.352	0.00
SO	St. Petersburg (Original)	7.330	6.352	0.000	21.682	0.33
SM	Seminole	3.000	6.352	0.000	17.592 TD	0.00
TI	Treasure Island	4.120	6.352	0.000	18.472	0.00
TF	Tarpon Springs FID ...	0.000	7.707	3.100	19.047 TD	0.00
TS	Tarpon Springs	4.658	6.352	0.000	19.250 TD	0.00
WLTD	Whispering LT, TR ...	0.210	7.707	0.000	16.157 TD	0.00

Total Millage is made up of:
A. 8.000 mills set by Pinellas County School Board
B. 5.655 mills set by Board of County Commissioners
   1. 2.835 mills .... general fund
   2. 0.121 mills .... road fund
   3. 0.987 mills .... capital improvement
   4. 0.133 mills .... mosquito control
   5. 0.242 mills .... health department
   6. 0.135 mills .... debt service
   7. 1.202 mills .... sewer construction
     5.655
C. 0.697 mills set by other taxing authorities
   1. 0.392 mills .... Juvenile Welfare Board
   2. 0.005 mills .... West Coast Inland Navigation District
   3. 0.120 mills .... Pinellas-Anclote River Basin
   4. 0.030 mills .... Pinellas County Planning Council
   5. 0.150 mills .... Southwest Florida Water Management District
     0.697
     6.352 total millage countywide
D. 1.355 mills for Municipal Service Taxing District (MSTD)
E. City or district (including lighting, transit, and fire) millage

8. The ownership roll shows any and all exemptions from taxes payable, and identifies the type of exemption. This is a convenient way of identifying, for example, nonresident owners (no homestead exemption) or resident owners who neglected to file for an exemption.

Alphabetical Index

The sequence of data in both property maps and ownership rolls is geographic. However, not every inquiry concerning property starts with a parcel number, a legal description, a subdivision name, or some other easy identifier.

Some situations start off with a comment like this, "I hear that someone named Wolfe—his first name is either Glenn or Geoffrey— is trying to sell his house himself. It's on the North side, I think." In such a situation, the real estate salesperson may refer to an alphabetical index, which is a complete roster of each and every real property owner in a county.

SAMPLE ALPHABETICAL INDEX
(listed alphabetically by owner's name)

Owner's Name		Assessor's Parcel Number	Taxing District
WOLFE	GEORGE H ◆ RUTH A	64032-18-007	11C
WOLFE	GEORGIA C	64304-04-013	C2D
WOLFE	GLENN C ◆ MARTHA B	74253-06-002	12M
WOLFE	JERRY L ◆ PATRICIA A	63322-04-009	11S

The Alpha immediately links the owner (by name) with the parcel or parcels (by number) that he or she owns. The parcel number can then be used to research the ownership roll for other vital details, such as the owner's address, the assessed value of the property, and exemptions. The agent may refer to the Alpha to see whether a prospect owns other properties in the county. Those properties may be also available for sale. Determining what other properties a prospect owns will also give the real estate salesperson a better picture of the prospect's purchasing strength. The Alpha can also be researched to identify specialty investors (for example, triplex buyers) to advise them of a newly listed like property.

The Situs Index

If a real estate salesperson knows the address of a property but does not know the owner's name, the property can be linked with its owner by means of the situs index, which lists property alphabetically by street name.

SAMPLE SITUS INDEX
(listed alphabetically by street name)

Street Name			
Street Address			
Assessor's Parcel Number			
Taxing District			

```
SNYDER AVE   03025        64032-20-003   11C
SNYDER AVE   02028        64032-19-012   11C
SNYDER AVE   02102        64032-19-009   11C
SNYDER AVE   02106        64032-19-008   11C
SNYDER AVE   02110        64032-19-005   11C
SNYDER AVE   02114        64032-19-004   11C
SNYDER AVE   02122        64032-19-001   11C
```

Realty Sales Service (RSS)

The real estate salesperson also needs to be able to answer these questions:

1. Is the owner of record (as of the last tax roll release date) still the owner? If not, who is?
2. What are properties selling for in a given area, and/or what did a specific property sell for?

FIGURE 4–9
Sample Realty Sales Service

Cumulative Dates

Published Date

Official Records Book & Page

Acreage & Unrecorded Plats

Indicates Current Month's Sale

Deed Type Code

Township, Range & Section

Buyer's Name & Mailing Address

Subdivision Name

Seller's Name

Subdivision Block & Lot

Sale Price

Lender's Name

Plat Book & Page

Instrument Date

Amount of New Mortgage

Atlas Page Number

FIGURE 4–10
Sample RSS for Condominiums

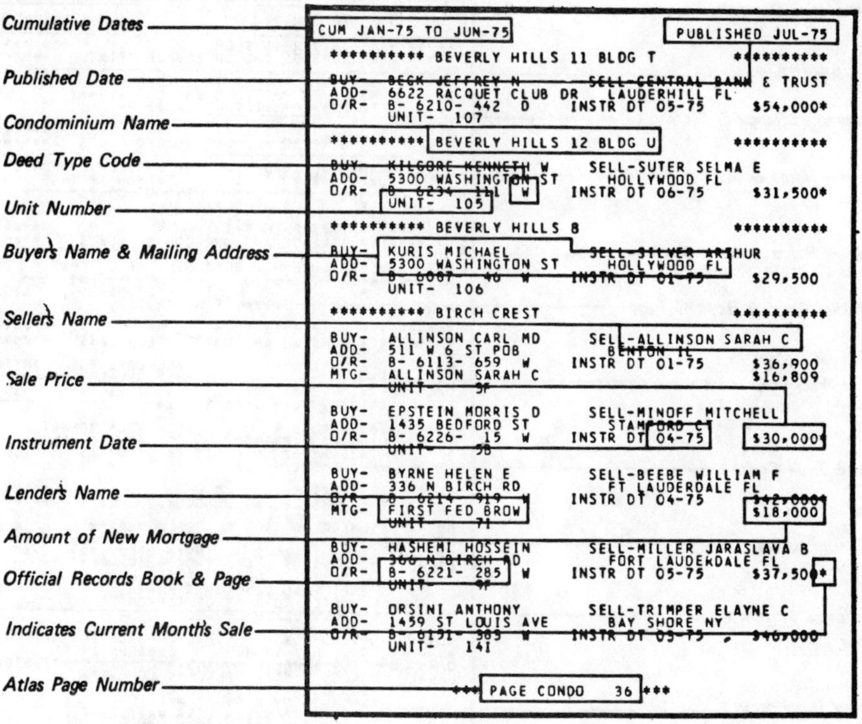

Cumulative Dates
Published Date
Condominium Name
Deed Type Code
Unit Number
Buyer's Name & Mailing Address
Seller's Name
Sale Price
Instrument Date
Lender's Name
Amount of New Mortgage
Official Records Book & Page
Indicates Current Month's Sale
Atlas Page Number

REDI's Realty Sales Service furnishes the real estate salesperson with a monthly cumulative report on all real estate transactions that occurred in a given area, including all subdivision, condominium, and acreage sales (see Figures 4–9, 4–10, and 4–11).

1. The RSS brings the ownership roll up-to-date on an ongoing basis.

2. The RSS is geographically oriented so that property transactions can be tracked by area (a given subdivision, for example) and by type (condominiums, for example).

3. The RSS cumulative data indicate trends which can be detected.

4. The RSS identifies, by area and property type, the active buyers and sellers. A real estate salesperson can scan each new issue to see "what's happening" in an area, just as an investor can scan the *Wall Street Journal* to see what's happening on the market.

5. The RSS can help a listor to recover an otherwise lost commission by identifying listings sold without his or her knowledge.

FIGURE 4–11
Sample RSS for Acreage

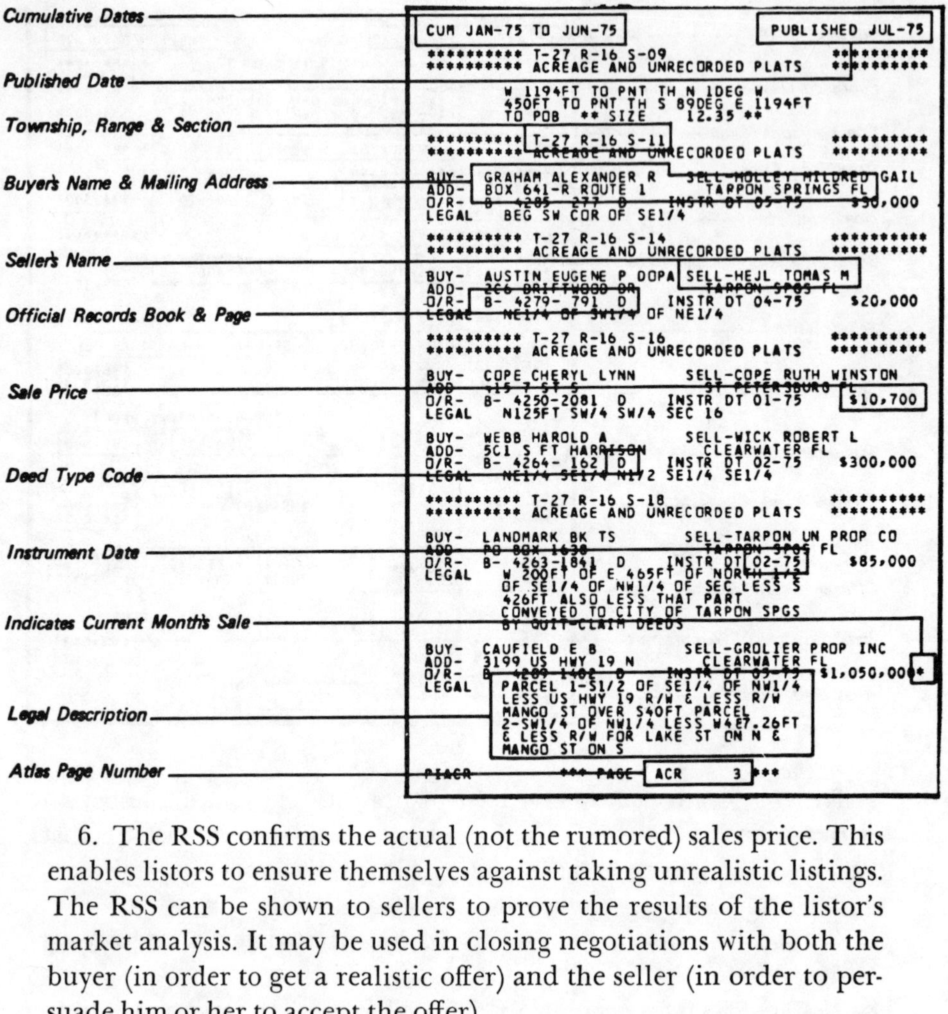

Cumulative Dates	
Published Date	
Township, Range & Section	
Buyer's Name & Mailing Address	
Seller's Name	
Official Records Book & Page	
Sale Price	
Deed Type Code	
Instrument Date	
Indicates Current Month's Sale	
Legal Description	
Atlas Page Number	

```
CUM JAN-75 TO JUN-75                    PUBLISHED JUL-75
********** T-27 R-16 S-09        **********
********** ACREAGE AND UNRECORDED PLATS  **********
          W 1194FT TO PNT TH N 1DEG W
          450FT TO PNT TH S 89DEG E 1194FT
          TO POB  ** SIZE    12.35 **
********** T-27 R-16 S-11        **********
********** ACREAGE AND UNRECORDED PLATS  **********
BUY- GRAHAM ALEXANDER R    SELL-MOLLEY MILDRED GAIL
ADD- BOX 641-R ROUTE 1          TARPON SPRINGS FL
O/R- B- 4205 277 D     INSTR DT 05-75     $30,000
LEGAL   BEG SW COR OF SE1/4
********** T-27 R-16 S-14        **********
********** ACREAGE AND UNRECORDED PLATS  **********
BUY- AUSTIN EUGENE P DOPA SELL-HEJL TOMAS M
ADD- 266 DRIFTWOOD DR         TARPON SPGS FL
O/R- B- 4279 791 D     INSTR DT 04-75     $20,000
LEGAL   NE1/4 OF SW1/4 OF NE1/4
********** T-27 R-16 S-16        **********
********** ACREAGE AND UNRECORDED PLATS  **********
BUY- COPE CHERYL LYNN     SELL-COPE RUTH WINSTON
ADD- 415 7 ST S           ST PETERSBURG FL
O/R- B- 4250-2081 D    INSTR DT 01-75     $10,700
LEGAL   N125FT SW/4 SW/4 SEC 16
BUY- WEBB HAROLD A        SELL-WICK ROBERT L
ADD- 5C1 S FT HARRISON        CLEARWATER FL
O/R- B- 4264- 162 D    INSTR DT 02-75    $300,000
LEGAL   NE1/4 SE1/4 N1/2 SE1/4 SE1/4
********** T-27 R-16 S-18        **********
********** ACREAGE AND UNRECORDED PLATS  **********
BUY- LANDMARK BK TS       SELL-TARPON UN PROP CO
ADD- PO BOX 1636              TARPON SPGS FL
O/R- B- 4263-1861 D    INSTR DT 02-75     $85,000
LEGAL   W 200FT OF E 465FT OF NORTH 1/2
        OF SE1/4 OF NW1/4 OF SEC LESS S
        426FT ALSO LESS THAT PART
        CONVEYED TO CITY OF TARPON SPGS
        BY QUIT-CLAIM DEEDS
BUY- CAUFIELD E B         SELL-GROLIER PROP INC
ADD- 3199 US HWY 19 N         CLEARWATER FL
O/R- B- 4209-1102 D    INSTR DT 05-75  $1,050,000 **
LEGAL   PARCEL 1-S1/2 OF SE1/4 OF NW1/4
        LESS US HWY 19 R/W & LESS R/W
        MANGO ST OVER S40FT PARCEL
        2-SW1/4 OF NW1/4 LESS W487.26FT
        & LESS R/W FOR LAKE ST ON N &
        MANGO ST ON S
**ACR      *** PAGE  ACR    3  ***
```

6. The RSS confirms the actual (not the rumored) sales price. This enables listors to ensure themselves against taking unrealistic listings. The RSS can be shown to sellers to prove the results of the listor's market analysis. It may be used in closing negotiations with both the buyer (in order to get a realistic offer) and the seller (in order to persuade him or her to accept the offer).

7. The RSS mortgage information identifies lenders by area, neighborhood, and activity. It can be used to analyze the ratio of loans to sales price in order to obtain the best type of loans (FHA, VA, conventional) for the client.

The Appraiser's Handbook

In counties where it is available, the *Appraiser's Handbook* is especially helpful to the listor. Notice that an improvement code is

FIGURE 4-12
Sample *Appraiser's Handbook* Listing (listed numerically by assessor's schedule number)

Assessor's Schedule Number
Property Address
Property Classification
Improvement Code
Year Built
Zoning Code
Land Line Code
Date of Sale
Sale Price
Land Square Footage
Building Square Footage
Deed Book & Page
Type of Instrument
Fair Market Land Value
Fair Market Improvement Value

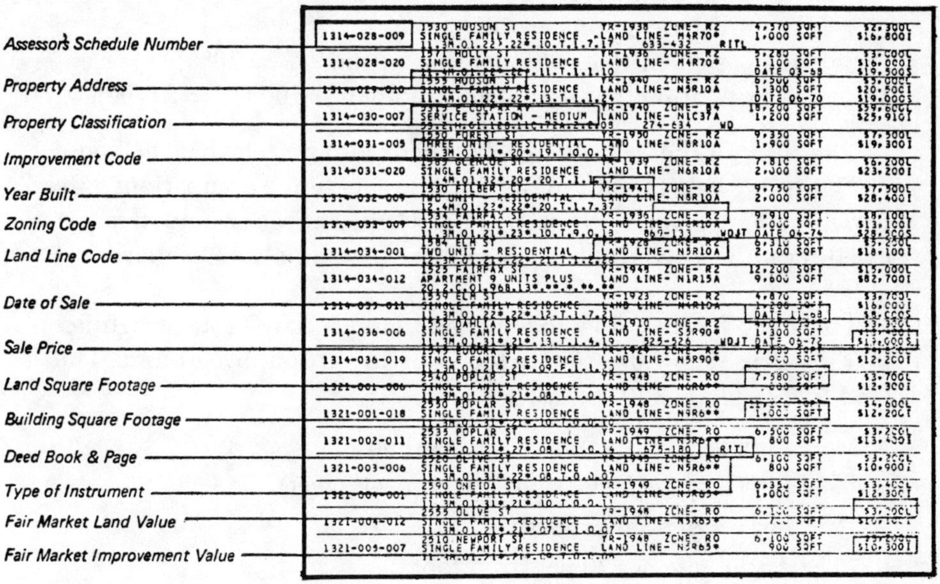

indicated for each entry in Figure 4–12. For example, the property at "1530 Hudson St." is coded as follows:

11.3M. 01.22*.10.T.1.7.17

Decoded according to REDI's explanation and use booklet, the property at 1530 Hudson Street:

1. Is a residence (1).
2. Is for a single family (1).
3. Is of average quality (3).
4. Is constructed of brick (M = masonry).
5. Contains one building (01).
6. Has two bedrooms (2).
7. Has two baths (2).
8. Was built by an unknown builder (*). If this were a newer property, a letter would indicate the builder.
9. Is a one-story structure (2 = 1 story, 3 = 1½ story, and so on).
10. Has a two-car garage (2).
11. Has not been identified as to model*. If this were a newer property, the model of the house would be indicated.

12. Has 1,000 square feet of living area on the first floor (10).
13. Is "typical" of the area (T).
14. Has a full basement (1 = 100%).
15. Has a basement that is 70 percent finished (7 = 70%).
16. Has a valuation that should add another $1,700 (17 = $1700).

The entry in the *Appraiser's Handbook* also reveals that the house was built in 1938. The R2 zoning means that "home occupations" are permitted and that a minimum of 3,000 square feet of land area per dwelling unit is required. This property contains 4,570 square feet of land.

The 1,000 figure below the entry on land square footage signifies that the house has 1,000 square feet of living area aboveground. The land line code M4R70 means:

M = A module was applied in the valuation.

4 = For frontage feet (from 35 feet to 44.9 feet).

R = For residential property.

70 = At the rate of $70 per front foot.

The figure 633–432 and the code RITL below the land line entry signify that on page 432 of Deed Book 633 a release of inheritance tax lien has been recorded.

The land value and the improvement (building) value are $2,300 and $16,800, respectively.

It should be readily evident that the *Appraiser's Handbook* is particularly useful in older neighborhoods whose homes were not built by one builder and therefore cannot be identified according to model number. If the real-estate salesperson's broker leases such a volume, the salesperson may research a property *before* going to the home to discuss a listing. By comparing the improvement code and other items with those for similar properties, the listor may be able to prepare a market analysis before ever seeing the property.

REDI is equipped to perform feasibility studies, economic trend studies, land use analysis, market potential studies, site location analysis, and other custom real estate research.

HOW? (CONTINUED)

Top farm listors agree that after selecting a farm area, the next step is to inspect the area.

"The first thing to do," says Don Nourse, "is to get in your car with a legal pad, drive through the entire area, and write down every street name and every address."

Second, Don advises, return to your office and get the names of the occupants at each address and the other available information about the property (legal description, lot size, and so on).

And be certain, he continues, to note whether any of the occupants are merely tenants. "Bombard those out-of-area owners with mail, because those are the people who are going to sell the houses. Make sure to do that, no matter what. And also mail special items to the tenants about buying a house versus renting a house."

Third, duplicate maps of the area. Also, find out what company built the subdivision. Go to the company and get a sequence sheet which shows the floor plan for each house. If this is not possible, you may be able to obtain the same information by using the REDI *Appraiser's Handbook* (if one for your area is available) or by going to the assessor's office and reviewing the property record card. And every time you list a house, ask the owners whether they have a copy of the floor plan. Otherwise, prepare your own.

Next, get copies of the deeds.

"Now this is a lot of work," emphasizes Don. "Very few people will do this. I'll tell them step by step what to do—it will only take them two weeks of good hard work—and you know, they just won't do it. They'll go to the directories, get the names opposite the address, and then they quit. So then they are sending 500 cards out, and maybe 30 percent of the cards get to the people and the rest go into the trash. The directories are good, but *all* information has to be updated. Even though my records are accurate, I must work on them every week."

Develop a card for every house, by street, with all the pertinent information you have secured. Show the date the house sells and the price at which it sells. Indicate the model number of the house or use the improvement code in the REDI *Appraiser's Handbook*. This will assist you in rapidly selecting comparables.

Then, if a client is interested in a particular type of property, you can easily go through your file and select by code those properties which meet the client's specifications. If you have a buyer coming into town, you may want to telephone 20 or 30 people. "I have a buyer coming in from such and such a town. Are you interested in selling your home?" Using this method, you know precisely whom to call.

" 'This is Don Nourse. I know you own a Plan 4, which is that really nice, large four-bedroom home with 2½ baths. I have a great buyer coming in from _____. And I'm just calling owners of this plan to see if anyone is interested in selling.' This causes the seller to think, 'This real estate salesperson knows what I have, knows my house.' So even if he doesn't sell his house now, he's going to know that I know what I'm talking about."

A listor may also obtain a picture of each property. If he is unable to cut a picture out of his multilist book, he can take his own snapshot. "If a buyer walks in, there's nothing better than pulling out a complete file on a home, with descriptions and pictures. The client begins to feel more comfortable and knows he's not dealing with an incompetent."

But the effect upon sellers is just as great. If Nourse has difficulty in convincing a seller of the fair market value of his home, he just opens his file and lets the seller see its contents and his comparables. "I have this information on every home. I've seen every house that has sold in here. And this is what your house is worth."

Both Bloomquist and Nourse caution real estate salespersons to work hard and fast in obtaining the preparatory information. Says Bloomquist, "I've seen people who want to work a farm, and they spend six months getting ready." By then, they may be out of the real estate business. If they have not given up, they have spent so much time accumulating information about their prospects that they have never had time to go out and meet them. It is important to know your prospects and even more important for them to know you.

"I knock on doors every 60 days," explains Dan. "There is a constant maintenance program. The owners will forget you if you don't keep after them.

"If the real estate salesperson lives in an area, and likes the area, and is willing to do a better job than the other persons who are working it, he should be able to clobber the competition. It would be nice to find an area where no one is working, but that is probably just not possible.

"Before I started working Queensborough, an agent for _____ Realty had been getting most of the listings for two years. But he would never knock on doors. He would only send out mailings once in a while. He got quite a bit of the business because he happened to live in the area. But when I started knocking on doors and sending out mail, he gradually got less and less. I don't think he gets more than a handful of listings now—at most."

Dan's farm is not an area with a lot of organizations. "My people are an eight to five group. I suppose if I worked an area of $70,000 homes, it might be important to belong to a lot of organizations."

Dan points out three things that are necessary for a successful farm program.

1. *Exposure.*   You have to know every homeowner. And they have to know you. Exposure is accomplished by knocking on doors and by a regular, systematic mail program. "The fact that my farm listings increased from 36 percent in 1974 to 49 percent in 1975 was due, I believe, to the mail campaign I started in late 1974."

Nourse stresses the importance of having an accurately prepared mailing list and a systematic mail program.

Every person in Dan Bloomquist's and Don Nourse's farms gets a piece of literature every single month.

Twice a year Don sends out a special letter. Each month he mails a postcard. And he advertises in community newspapers.

The details of these mail and advertising programs will be noted in Chapter 6.

2. *Persistence.*   Have a program and stay with it.

In connection with this trait, it is worth noting a passage attributed to Grover Cleveland:

Press On

Nothing in the world can take the place of persistence.

Talent will not: Nothing is more common than unsuccessful men with talent.

Genius will not: Unrewarded genius is almost a proverb.

Education alone will not: The world is full of educated derelicts.

Persistence and determination alone are omnipotent.

3. *Reputation.*   You must be certain that the listings you take are priced right so that they are salable. "People watch those signs. If you get two or three that don't sell, particularly when you are beginning," warns Bloomquist, "that'll kill you. But if what you list is selling, and you combine that with your canvassing and your mailings, you can develop a good, strong reputation."

Working a real estate *farm* is like working an agricultural farm:

You must select and survey the area.

You must, with proper tools, plow the ground, uncovering and learning about every inch of the area.

You must plant the seeds by getting out and spreading around your identity, your knowledge, and your skill.

You must cultivate and maintain your farm, never letting your initial efforts turn to weeds.

Do these things, and you will reap a rich harvest.

5

The Associational Farm

The immediate reaction of those hearing the expression *real estate farm* is to think of a geographic area comprising perhaps 500 to 600 homes which a real estate salesperson solicits regularly for the purpose of securing business.

SOURCES

However, another source of listings might be referred to as the *associational farm*. This term refers to listings generated as a result of the real estate salesperson's activities and associations with relatives, friends, social and business contacts, and former clients.

Mike Knapp believes that most agents obtain listings the hard way, by pounding the streets and outsparring one another. As far as he is concerned, it is a lot easier for the real estate salesperson to build up a clientele that will notify him or her of their plans than it is for the real estate salesperson to seek out prospective sellers.

"Begin by relying on your friends," suggests Mike. "Most salespeople just don't realize how many people they already know. Practically everywhere I go the topic of real estate comes up in conversations. I may be out with friends who have friends about to make a move. I had a woman phone me about an hour ago. I met her when she and her husband contacted me about one of my listings. After I sold them a house, we became friends. About six months ago a friend of this couple was transferred. As a result of their recommendation, I listed his house. Now they have other friends who are moving. She called to give me their names because they want me to list their home."

Repeats and referrals have been the prime source of listings for Everett Sanburn, newly appointed managing broker of the Gresham office of E. J. Pounder Realty Company, Portland Oregon. "Why slave to cultivate new people when the people you already know will cultivate about as much business as you can handle?"

Sanburn emphasizes that the seed from one referral can grow into a giant money tree. It is true, he points out, that some referrals are like dead ends—they go no place. And there are people who would not tell you if your own brother were selling his house. On the other hand, there are others who will scour the city on your behalf. As far as they are concerned, nothing is too good for you. "So which ones do I cultivate? Naturally, I cultivate those who will grow so that I will grow with them.

"Just work hard for the leads you get and take very good care of the leads you already have. A lot of salespeople spend a lot of time and money and effort trying to run down a new prospect when they already have clients who know they are good. As far as I am concerned, it is ridiculous to forget to cultivate those clients."

In agreement with Sanburn's emphasis on referral business, Jim Kunkel says, "It is surprising how you can develop maybe a dozen clients who will send you 50 to 70 percent of your business. Last year I obtained more than 50 percent of my business from six or seven people. And it snowballs. From those referrals I obtained further referrals. People who have complete confidence and trust in my knowledge, honesty, and experience keep an eye out for me."

"A geographic farm territory is too limiting for me," says Gary Shapiro. "My farm becomes the people I have met through my club affiliations, volunteer work, and civic projects."

From his very first day in business, Gary has completed a follow-up card on everyone with whom he has developed an association (Figure 5-1).

"Just the follow-up to keep in touch with the clients of my $4 million worth of active listings, plus the escrows I maintain, the turnover, and my mailing program, keeps my personal secretary and me busy probably 14 hours a day," says Gary.

Among the various types of people with whom one may associate in order to develop a referral system are architects, designers, planners,

FIGURE 5–1
Follow-up Card for an Associational Farm

Name _____ Wife _____
Street _____
City _____ State _____ Zip _____
(H) _____ (O) _____
Employ _____
Source _____ Year _____
Kids _____
M B-day _____ W B-day _____ Anv _____
R.E. Activity _____
_____
_____
_____
_____
_____

and interior decorators. Such people can refer business to real estate salespersons since they often have advance notice of people's intentions to build, buy, or sell.

Rosemary Kane explains that initially she joined community organizations that would enable her to meet homeowners. And many of her former clients have become close friends. "I also developed friends among business people. One of them is an interior decorator who sends me a great number of referrals. And, of course, I reciprocate."

Almost all attorneys handle some real estate transactions for their clients. The disposition of estates because of death and divorce, for instance, can provide a great number of referrals.

Mike Silverman of Silverman and Associates, Beverly Hills, California, repeats what he recently told Mike Wallace on CBS's "60 Minutes" program. "A big source of real estate business for my company is the high divorce rate. For the successful real estate agent, each divorce translates into a house for sale and conceivably two or more houses to be bought."

Insurance salespersons also know a good deal about their clients' plans, as do tax consultants and accountants. Members of these latter professions are outstanding sources of business since they are directly concerned with the sale, refinancing, or exchange of their clients' real estate. And this is particularly true in the case of investment properties wherein tax and depreciation factors affect the need to buy and sell property.

At one time David McGinnis had few connections among business people, yet felt he needed them. He recalls that while taking management courses in college, he studied the "sphere of influence" concept. This concept and his need for business referrals caused him to start a TIPS club.

The club is made up of one representative only from each of a number of different occupations: an insurance salesperson, a stockbroker, a banker, a lawyer, a real estate salesperson, a person in advertising, and a few people who own different types of retail stores.

Dave looked for young people like himself who were starting out in business and needed someone to help them obtain leads and tips. The club started out slowly but has since become very effective because the capacities of each of its members have grown.

For example, as Dave points out, the attorney was a law clerk when the club was founded, but now owns his own firm. Through him, Dave obtains a great number of leads that originate in divorces, property settlements, estate settlements, and the like.

Because a lot of people check with their insurance salesperson before selling their homes, Dave has been able to obtain leads from the TIPS insurance member.

TIPS members receive no money for their leads—just reciprocal assistance. The club's members have breakfast together every two weeks. They talk over general business conditions in the area. And whenever information becomes available, they share leads with one another.

"It is amazing how well this system works," exclaims Dave. "I had a client who came to me from out-of-state and therefore knew very few people in the community. I sold him a home. The TIPS attorney did his legal work. The TIPS insurance man handled all his insurance. The TIPS member who owns a fuel oil business took care of his fuel needs. And the TIPS man who has a carpeting store recarpeted his house.

"TIPS has probably benefited me more than anything else I have done. The help of its members has been tremendous. It's like having a dozen or so people working for me all the time at no charge. The leads just keep pouring in."

Former business associates have been a solid source of referrals for Paul Manners of Mile-Hi Realty, Cheyenne, Wyoming, and for Harry

Polay of Gifford Realty, Norfolk, Virginia. As Harry remarks, "My centers of influence have been in the business community in which I was active for some 22 years. I don't specifically have to court these people. They just come to me."

Most builders do not have their own sales organizations and therefore need real estate sales representation. Custom builders are especially in need of such representation since their market is limited to a small segment of the total housing field. They need greater exposure to reach their select clientele.

For this reason, Mike Knapp has developed an associational farm with builders. "You list and sell a house of theirs. Then you go back for another listing or two. You sell one of those and go back for two or three listings. There is no special way to approach builders other than to be sympathetic to their way of thinking and to put yourself in their position. The most important thing is to establish a reputation for doing a good job for them. They will then advertise you among their fellow builders."

Merchants with whom real estate salespersons and their families do business can be valuable centers of influence. They can refer or direct you to a lot of business if you ask them for it and let them know you are interested in receiving it.

For Nila Laman such a center of influence is the owner of the market where she has traded for the past 12 years. He has bought five houses from her. His employees, knowing that he has bought from Nila, have also sold through her and bought from her. In addition, as a center of information, he has furnished her with innumerable leads.

Dave Webster's associational farm has become the fire fighters in the Norfolk, Chesapeake, and Virginia Beach areas of Virginia. "I handle the bulk of the business for the Norfolk fire fighters," says Webster. "The 'in' I have with these people is the source of about 60 percent of my business. They are buying and selling in these three cities all the time. I go to all of them."

Since banks and their trust departments handle properties for clients, Austin Baker of Clover Realty, Atlanta, has this associational farm as a source of referrals.

The wise listor will also consider cultivating savings and loan associations and mortgage companies. You can bring business to them, and they can reciprocate by giving you referrals. In addition, they often use the services of real estate salespersons themselves in disposing of foreclosed properties.

Rick Niday has developed an associational farm among the personnel officers of a number of companies. "I call on management once a week. I don't ask for business, but just make the contact to let them know I am still selling and buying real estate.

"I developed a referral business with Supervalue, a national food chain, when I listed the property of the head of the company. I asked who was replacing him. And when he told me, I contacted that individual and sold him a house. One thing led to another, and now I handle all their business."

Associate broker Carole Kelby says that her referral business with Wilson and Company began when she listed a town house one Tuesday evening for an employee who had been told earlier in the day that he had been transferred and was to leave for California the following Sunday. The man had a wife, a nine-year-old child, a one-year-old child, and a two-month-old baby.

The wife, with big tears in her eyes, cried, "Please sell it quick. I don't want to stay here by myself." Carole sold the town house Thursday morning. It was a cash transaction. And the entire family was able to leave together the following Sunday.

Before leaving, the man promoted her within his company by declaring, "She's a real tiger! Go get her." When asked to come in, Carole explained to the personnel director that she would not only help sellers and buyers, but that she would also help with rentals, and would charge no commission for her rental work.

When asked why, she explained, "Because every renter is a potential buyer, and that's future business. If not this year, then next year. Or the renter may know a friend interested in selling."

"And now," says Carole, "I get business monthly from them. I handle everything: plane reservations, motel reservations, car rentals if a company car is not going to be used. I pick up the clients at the airport, spend the entire day with them, and take them to lunch and dinner." If a property is purchased, Carole takes her clients to the bank, helps them arrange for financing, and gets them an attorney to close.

Although Veloris J. Petersen is a top producer for Bermel Smaby Realty in Minneapolis, she says that real estate comes second. She explains this by noting that her real estate business evolves rather naturally from her involvement in various social, musical, and academic activities. At one time, she counseled in the adult education department at the University of Minnesota.

This counseling experience, plus her singing, her musical and cultural activities, and her interests in the community, has enabled her to develop an associational farm among attorneys, physicians, professors, and musicians.

Lucy Ann Bell admits that it was a matter of "getting my face in front of the people and getting them to realize I was in the real estate business." She belongs to the Junior League and the Beach Club. "My mother is very active socially. She started many of the major philanthropic groups in town. And so a lot of my success, I'm sure, has to do with her reputation."

Mike Silverman advises that "a social whirl pays off. Most of our contacts arise out of social circumstances. Just meeting someone in real estate may trigger the principal's brain. 'Say, our house is too small. Why don't you talk to us about getting a bigger house?'

"The mere fact that the agent is in view generates all sorts of questions from people about real estate, questions which evolve into listings. Many of our people have been in show business. For example, Ed Kelly, vice president of our company, was Peggy Lee's personal manager for ten years."

The value of developing an associational farm among former clients is illustrated by Colleen Rosinbum. Noting how difficult it is to keep in touch with former clients and referrals, Colleen remarked, "I just had a call from a man to whom I sold a property some four years ago when I was with another real estate broker. He had purchased a home for his two sons, who were attending the university. I had forgotten all about him. Yet he recently phoned my former company. Someone there told him I was now associated with another broker. He phoned me here and asked if I would list and sell that house."

SERVICING

All the top listors agree that properly servicing a listing is essential in developing a solid referral business.

Dave McGinnis says, "It is important to keep the seller informed. If you put in an ad, call the owners and tell them about it. And send them a copy. If you do a superb job getting a listing, but afterward never let the sellers know what you are doing and what is happening, then you lose the benefits of your listing efforts."

Sarah Catherine Holley believes that, by properly servicing her listings, she is able to get additional listings. She visits the owners of her listings every other week. "If I have 15, that means I have to contact one seller every day. Each month I give my sellers a report of all the houses in their area that have sold—the price, the terms, and how the price relates to their price on a square foot basis. This lets the sellers know right away if their house is overpriced."

Carole Kelby remarks that in servicing her listings she does "a couple of extra things that most real estate salespersons don't do. First of all, I have my own full-time secretary. Every Monday I have her phone each of my listings to find out who has shown the property over the weekend. In our area, other brokers are permitted to make direct arrangements for showings. After contacting each salesperson, my secretary shares the feedback she got with the owner.

"On Friday, she repeats the service for owners whose homes have been shown since Monday. In this way, my homeowners are kept abreast of market reaction. If I have a seller who is really unhappy because his home hasn't been sold, rather than have him call me, I phone him every day. He knows I am interested. He knows I care. And he knows I am trying to get him the best price I can."

After the settlement is completed, and while his clients are still at the closing table, Dave McGinnis asks them whether he may use their names as a reference. "This has worked wonders. Especially here in Burlington. We are a big IBM town, and the employees tend to stick together. I make it a practice to say, 'Please call this person. Here is his phone number. He works in this office. We sold his house a few months ago, and he was in a situation like yours and was satisfied. Please phone him.' And they do. I have had good results with that method."

Eunice Reass attributes the strength of her referral program to the fact that she never forgets anyone and that she always stands behind her sales. "If a dishwasher or a disposal broke down after the sale, I always felt that repairing or replacing it was to my benefit. It solved lots of hassles. Everyone knew that I stood behind what I sold, and my sellers were always happy because I didn't 'bug' them about such problems after a transaction closed. Accordingly, they recommended me to other people."

Lee Burch is certain that the volume of her repeat business is a result of her constant follow-up program. "You just cannot list and sell a piece of property and think those people will come back to you. I have a program which has been very successful."

Each time Mrs. Burch closes a transaction, she makes a 3 × 5 card on the purchase. She lists the date on which the person bought the house. "This purchaser is usually my repeat listing. Also, if his or her next-door neighbor decides to sell, my purchaser will say, 'Well, I bought my house from Lee Burch. And I was very happy with her service.' "

Lee's follow-up file, which she maintains religiously, is set up according to name and then cross-filed by street address. Each time she does something for the purchaser or is in touch with him or her she records that in her file. When the purchaser moves in, Lee prepares a 3 × 5 "Thank-You Gram" in which she thanks him for his business in a handwritten note.

Each March, Lee sends out mortgage exemption reminders. "In our state we have a $1,000 mortgage exemption that applies to anyone who owns property with a mortgage of $1,000 or more. This exemption saves such property owners about $100 per year. So I send my purchasers a little mortgage exemption card printed by our company. The only thing they need to do is add a postage stamp. My accompanying note reminds them to file the card between March 1 and May 1."

At Thanksgiving, Lee sends a plant to all first-year prospects and to those with whom she has done business. "This seems to be regarded as a real fine token of appreciation. Almost everyone gets something at Christmas. But at Thanksgiving, when the family is together, a gift seems to be much more important."

On December 1, Mrs. Burch furnishes an attractive wall-hung cloth calendar. She tries to deliver these personally. "It's amazing how people who have not yet received one will call me. 'I haven't received your calendar this year. Did you forget?'

"Of course, I mail out Christmas cards. I've been told that is foolish. But I continue because too often I've gotten listings from people who say, 'You never forgot me at Christmastime.' "

If Lee gets in a slump, she pulls out her card file and starts calling people, asking them how they are and how they are getting along in their new home. Often they will tell her, "Say, I know some people who are going to sell their home."

"Even though you have been in the business as long as I have, you have to constantly work on your follow-ups. If you keep in regular contact with these people, when you do make an occasional phone call to get business, it is not regarded as anything out of the ordinary. But you cannot just give people gifts. You must show your concern for them by contacting them with a personal visit or a phone call."

The associational farm—the specific group of individuals with whom the real estate salesperson maintains regular and systematic contact—is thus another potent source of listings for top real estate salespeople.

6

Media

A real estate salesperson cannot be like the Wizard of Oz who secluded himself behind a screen and manipulated the actions of thousands.

Remember, obtaining listings is no different from applying for any other job. The listor must convince the homeowner of his need for a real estate salesperson and of his need for this particular real estate salesperson.

At some time or other, therefore, it is necessary for listors to confront their prospective employers face-to-face.

Nevertheless, there are tools which real estate salespersons may use effectively to aid them in locating listings and in maintaining their profile before the selling public with a view toward future employment. Among these tools, the top listors make great use of the mails, the telephone, and advertising—*as aids* to their overall marketing program.

THE MAILS

A systematic mail program keeps the name of the real estate salesperson before the public. It also enables the listor to reach many people quickly and inexpensively. If you calculate the real estate salesperson's worth per hour, plus automobile costs, it is quite evident that spending 13 cents for postage and 3 cents for a sheet of paper and an envelope is a comparatively inexpensive way of keeping in touch with someone. The postman is going that way anyway. You might as well take advantage of his service.

The top listors all agree that the ingredients for success include knowledge plus face-to-face contact plus a systematic mail program.

As noted earlier, Dan Bloomquist is convinced that a year's monthly mailings in his farm were substantially responsible for increasing his business by 13 percent.

A systematic mail program "is crucial," according to Don Nourse. "The first day I started, I began mailing out postcards every month in my farm. I use a postcard because people don't have to open it. They look at it . . . see my name and picture . . . and throw it in the trash can. They do this 12 times a year. I'm going to hit them one of those times when they're thinking about selling their house."

Every piece of mail Don sends out shows his picture and includes the words "Don Nourse, the Turtle Rock Specialist."

Emphasizing the importance of a systematic mail program, Don says, "I have people who think I'm their best friend because I send them a piece of mail every month. Old ladies call me on the phone to talk about their real estate because they get this thing in the mail from me. I walk into a party someplace, and they know who I am. I go to the tennis club, and they know who I am. They don't often run up and talk to me. But every once in a while they will come up and ask me about real estate."

The content of Don's postcard can consist of any piece of information, such as the address of a new listing in the farm.

Although many real estate salespersons disagree, Don does not recommend the use of a letter announcing that "Don Nourse is going to be the new Turtle Rock expert." He believes that "no one wants a *new expert*. And besides, up until you begin your barrage, they don't know whether or not they've seen you before."

In addition to his monthly postcard mailings, Don mails a letter twice a year which recaps all the houses he has listed and/or sold during that year. The letter mailed out after the first half of the year may show 30 houses.

At the end of the year Don mails out his second letter. That letter may show 67 houses. "People look at it, and it's devastating."

At the top of Don's letter is the statement "I've sold $5 million worth of property and 67 houses." Next appear the column headings "address," "listed by," and "sold by." After the address of each prop-

76

FIGURE 6–1
A Sample Mailing Piece

Tom Fannin and Associates

3233 NORTH 24TH STREET • PHOENIX, ARIZONA 85016 • (602) 956-5630

THOMAS N. FANNIN • President

As President of Tom Fannin & Associates, REALTORS, I am proud to announce that Gary Shapiro, of our Scottsdale office, has recently earned the designation of "Lifetime Member" of our Million Dollar Sales Club.

Gary has been associated with our firm since 1971. For the past four years, he has distinguished himself by selling in excess of one million dollars of residential property annually.

In November of 1975, Gary was selected by the National Association of REALTORS to speak at their national convention in San Francisco. This was a great tribute to the dedication, professionalism, and accomplishments that Gary has worked so hard to achieve.

I am proud to have Gary Shapiro on the Tom Fannin team. I appreciate those of you who have already had an opportunity to do business with Gary. I urge each of you to continue to think of Gary when you and your friends need help concerning real estate.

Thank you,

Tom Fannin

Thomas N. Fannin, President

February 1976

REALTORS

PHOENIX • SCOTTSDALE • TEMPE • MESA • PRESCOTT • SEDONA

FIGURE 6-1 (*continued*)

SHAPIRO RECOGNIZED AS NATIONAL AUTHORITY ON LISTINGS

SELECTED TO SPEAK AT 1975 REALTORS NATIONAL CONVENTION

real estate todayly
tuesday

Published daily by the **REALTORS® NATIONAL MARKETING INSTITUTE**
for registrants of the 68th Annual Convention of the NATIONAL ASSOCIATION OF REALTORS®
Headquarters 155 East Superior Street, Chicago, Illinois 60611, (312) 440-8000

PROGRAM SCHEDULE

TODAY'S SPEAKERS . .
What You're Here For: to "Meet the Experts"

SHAPIRO

GARY A. SHAPIRO of Tom Fannin & Assoc.,
Scottsdale, Ariz., is a member of the firm's
Lifetime Million Dollar Sales Club.

TUESDAY, November 11

RD Money-Making Morning Meeting: "How to Double
Listing Income" — Art Godi, Stockton, Calif.; Gary
Shapiro, Scottsdale, Ariz.

Valley Realtor To Speak For National Meet

Valley realtor Gary A. Shapiro
will speak at the National Association
of Realtors Convention in
San Francisco this month.

Shapiro, of Tom Fannin and
Associates Realtors, will speak on
"Securing and Servicing Residential
Real Estate Listings."

Shapiro, with the Fannin Realty
since 1971, was awarded top
salesman's honors for the Scottsdale
branch in 1974. He is also a
member of Fannin's Million Dollar
Sales Club.

A member of the Scottsdale
Board of Realtors, Shapiro is also
on the Phoenix Board of Realtors.
He was chairman of the Scottsdale
Young Realty Associates in 1974.

PHOENIX JEWISH NEWS—Page 5

November 14, 1975—

Shapiro to address Realtors

Gary A. Shapiro of Tom
Fannin and Associates has
been selected to speak at the
National Association of Realtors
Convention in San Francisco
in November. Shapiro
will speak on securing and
servicing residential real
estate listings.

Shapiro has been with
Fannin Realty since 1971. He
was honored as the firm's top
salesman for the Scottsdale
branch in 1974. In addition, he
has been a member of Fannin's
Million Dollar Sales Club
every year since 1972. Shapiro
is a member of the Scottsdale
Board of Realtors, and he was
chairman of the Scottsdale
Young Realty Associates in

Shapiro

Sat.,
Oct. 25, 1975

6 Scottsdale (Az.)
Daily Progress

Real Estate Briefs

1974. He is a graduate of Arizona
State University.

erty, Don puts his name under the appropriate column or columns. If someone else either listed or sold the property, Don enters the words *co-op broker*. But the overall impression of the reader is that the name "Don Nourse, Don Nourse, Don Nourse, Don Nourse . . ." is splattered all over the page.

Gary Shapiro sends a personalized mailing to his associational farm four times a year. "At this point in my career, I would say that nine out of ten of my listings come from this program of mailings."

One of Gary's mailings included a formal engraved announcement of his GRI designation. Another concerned his selection as a speaker at the 1975 convention of the National Association of Realtors® (see Figure 6–1).

Instead of sending gifts to members of his associational farm during the Christmas–New Year season, Gary decided to adopt a foster child in the name of all his clients (see Figure 6–2).

"I receive a letter monthly from this child in the Philippines," explains Gary. "Twice a year I plan to reproduce one of the child's letters and to mail it along with a picture showing how the child has progressed.

"The response has been overwhelming. The people are tickled to death that I am so thoughtful. The adoption has brought in a wealth of goodwill and additional referrals. Out of the 1,900 persons on my mailing list, only one gentleman objected. He sent me a letter saying he thought it was crude to exploit some helpless individual for the sake of building business."

Besides his four scheduled mailings, Gary regularly mails anniversary and birthday cards.

Gary cautions, "Mailings are effective only when they are used repeatedly. One-shot mailings to neighborhoods or people that don't know you are ineffective."

Although your letter will vary according to its purpose, certain guidelines should be followed in constructing an *effective* letter.

1. *Determine your purpose.* Is your letter to thank, to sell, to inform? Your letter must have unity. And unity is achieved by limiting your letter to one topic. Ask yourself, "Why am I writing this?"

Is your purpose to induce an owner to list his single-family residence with you, or is it to convince a renter that he should buy instead of squandering his monthly rent payment? Your answer determines how you will formulate the contents of the letter.

2. *Visualize the recipient of your letter.* Certainly what you say to

FIGURE 6–2
A Reason to Write

GARY SHAPIRO
Tom Fannin & Associates, REALTORS ®
4841 North Scottsdale Road
Scottsdale, Arizona 85251

Dear Friend,

It is customary at this time of year for each of us to reflect on how fortunate we really are.

I have been blessed with many friends, business associates, and clients like you. During the past 5½ years, these people have been instrumental in helping me achieve personal and career goals.

In past holiday seasons, I spent considerable time and money on cards and token momentos that served to express my appreciation to people like you.

This year, I have decided to adopt a foster child on behalf of my clients and friends through the Foster Parents Plan, Inc.

It is my feeling that this support of a needy child better serves the "true holiday spirit" and demonstrates my genuine thankfulness for your friendship and goodwill.

Before proceeding with this adoption, I evaluated several options. Even though money for this program does not stay in the United States, I could not find a better program with more benefits. I welcome your suggestions that could be evaluated for future years.

I am excited that you and I will be able to help this needy child. Although I will bear all of the expense, I would like to share the joy of this program by sending you a copy of periodic letters from our foster child.

Thank you for making this possible. It has been another great year and I appreciate your continued patronage and support. I pledge that I will continue to give the best possible real estate service to you and your friends.

Happy Holidays!!!

Gary

December 1976

Member Million Dollar Sales Club

an elderly couple about to list their home so that they can retire to a condominium will differ from what you say to an owner of investment property.

3. *Begin your letter by catching the recipient's attention.* If you doubt the importance of this point, pick up a copy of *Reader's Digest* or any other successful magazine. Look at the title or the first few words of the articles. Scan the advertisements. These articles and ads were composed by people who earn their living gaining the attention of readers.

4. *Do not be extravagant or untruthful.* If you begin your letter with a startling statement, make sure that it is also a truthful statement. It's one thing to catch the reader's attention, but another to catch it with an exaggeration or a lie.

5. *Be brief.* The opening of your letter should hit the reader quickly like a boxer's jab to the face. Get right to the purpose. And keep the entire letter brief.

6. *Keep your paragraphs short.* A paragraph can be just one word. Or it can run on for sentence after sentence. As a rule, limit your paragraphs to three or four sentences. This is simply a matter of eye appeal.

7. *Structure your letter logically.* After indicating your purpose, give reasons in its support.

8. *Gain emphasis.* This may be accomplished by varying the length of your paragraphs. One-sentence paragraphs stand out from four-sentence paragraphs. They are therefore more emphatic.

The positioning of an idea within a sentence, a paragraph, or a letter determines its impact. People tend to grasp quickest and remember longest what is said at the beginning or the end of your letter and of its sentences and paragraphs.

9. *Use simple language.* Packing a letter full of big words will only turn the reader off. Use simple, meaningful words in a short and snappy fashion. Reveal to the reader that you are a bright, alert, and down-to-earth human being who is ready to do business.

10. *Close quickly. Time* magazine offers writers models of how to end an article. The same methods may be used to end a letter. Keep your last paragraph brief. Use it to restate your main point or to sum up the items you have stressed.

Typically, mail (letters, newsletters, postcards) will be used to:

1. Notify neighbors of a house just listed (Figure 6–3).

FIGURE 6-3
Notice to Neighbors of a House Just Listed

Dear

The owners of 1301 Elm have just appointed me to assist them in marketing their home.

In neighborhoods as nice as yours, very often homeowners have friends or relatives who wish to locate in the same neighborhood. Accordingly, I wish to call your attention to this home, which will afford an excellent opportunity for someone.

It is a well-kept 3 + 1 bedroom house with formal dining room, breakfast nook, 1¾ bath, full finished basement, recreation room, two fireplaces, and a two-car detached garage.

If you know of any people who wish to inspect this home, feel free to have them contact me for an immediate showing.

Sincerely,

P.S.   If ever you need anything notarized, don't hesitate to phone me.

2. Notify neighbors of a listed house that has just been sold (Figure 6–4).

FIGURE 6–4
Notice of a House Just Sold

Dear

Since only one buyer can purchase a particular property, we are often faced with the dilemma of "leftover" buyers.

Such is the situation in the East Central area around my listing at 720 Columbine, which I just recently sold and closed.

Speaking conservatively, I would say that I have at least 10 or 12 well-qualified buyers for this particular area, and I could quickly attract many more if only I had the property to show them.

Our real estate market has never been better! Values are high, and financing is readily available.

Could this be the time that you've been waiting for to sell your home? Or, would you possibly know of a neighbor or friend who is thinking of selling?

In either case, I would welcome your call for a prompt market analysis (no obligation, of course), a general discussion, or to simply answer any questions that you might have.

Sincerely,

3. Thank the sellers for the listing just given (Figure 6–5).

FIGURE 6–5
Expressing Appreciation for a New Listing

Dear

   Thank you for the confidence you have shown _____ Realty and me in permitting us to merchandise your home.

   Although I personally may be the one who will sell your home, my principal task will be to serve as a coodinator of these various marketing and closing transactions involved in selling your home.

   As I mentioned in our discussion, the four elements of a sucessful sale are (1) the price, (2) the financing terms available, (3) the condition of the property, and (4) salesmanship. Of the four, I have control only over the last.

   Regarding salemanship, I have included a commentary on advertising. Please take the time now to read it.

   Feel free to contact me at any time. It is my intention to make contact with you at least once a week.

                                        Sincerely,

4. Approach an FSBO (Figure 6–6). Note that the "selection factors" can be altered according to the size and particular characteristics of one's company.

FIGURE 6–6
Approaching an FSBO

Dear

You are attempting to sell your home yourself, most probably to avoid a broker's fee.

And there is absolutely no sarcasm when I say "I hope you are successful."

In the event, however, that one or more of the *four elements necessary* for a successful transaction are missing, perhaps you will decide that you need the assistance of a real estate broker.

Let me recommend that you be aware of several important factors when you make your selection.

a. Select a large company. A broker with 200 or more salespersons gets you the greatest exposure. He has hundreds upon hundreds of listings, and buyers contact the broker with the greatest selection. Second, since salespersons earn more commission selling their own company inventory, those 200 or more salespersons work diligently to sell your home. The smaller broker does not have enough properties to market, so he *also* will work on the listings of the larger broker, whereas the larger broker does not need to show the listings of the smaller broker.

b. Select an older company. As with many other things, age is a good test. A real estate broker who has been in business for many

FIGURE 6-6 (*continued*)

years has weathered the needs and the criteria of the community.

c. Select a full-service company. A real estate broker with his own mortgage and insurance companies and his own relocation service is better equipped to serve you and close those difficult sales.

d. Select a competent coordinator. Your coordinator within the company you select should be knowledgeable about appraising, financing, legal matters, merchandising, taxation, and more. A real estate salesperson who has the GRI designation is one who has completed a course of studies prescribed by the state Board of Realtors and meeting the minimum standards of the National Association of Realtors®.

May I point out that _____ Realty is a 44-year-old, full-service company with over 200 salespersons.

And finally, as a lifetime resident who holds the Graduate Realtor® Institute designation, I am convinced that I can effectively represent you. Within the past 12 months I have coordinated the closings of well over $_____ million of residential real estate in this area.

Please contact me if I may be of assistance to you.

Sincerely,

P.S.   Perhaps the enclosed information will help you.

5. Explain to neighbors that a house has come back on the market (Figure 6–7).

FIGURE 6–7
Announcing a House Back on the Market

Dear

Perhaps you have seen that the "For Sale" sign is again on the property at 120 South Chase Street. Very unfortunate circumstances prevented the prospective buyer from going through with the purchase.

I am enclosing an information sheet on this property for your review and assistance. Perhaps you know someone who might be interested in this fine home and whom you would like to have as a neighbor. We feel that this is an excellent buy.

If you have any suggestions for me, I would appreciate your comments. Thank you.

Very truly yours,

6. Follow up an out-of-town referral (Figure 6–8).

FIGURE 6–8
Following Up an Out-of-Town Referral

Dear

_____, your real estate broker in _____, has alerted us to the fact that you will be moving to _____ very soon. We know you will like it here, and it is a pleasure for us to be among the first to welcome you to this area.

In addition, I would like to offer my services—and those of the entire _____ realty organization—in helping you make this move as satisfying as possible. Our company has been active in _____ since _____. Our _____ conveniently located offices support a wide range of services for clients, including a force of _____ salespersons who handle a daily average of _____ exclusive listings throughout the _____ metropolitan area.

To help you know more about our city and our company, I have enclosed a brochure which I hope you will find interesting. If you have questions which the brochure does not answer, please let me know, and I will get the answers for you.

I can begin working on an early list of possible locations. This could save you some rather valuable time when you do arrive to look at homes and to complete the arrangements for your move.

We have helped thousands of families ease the pain of a major transfer by finding a home that's just right for them, and we can do the same for you.

I look forward to hearing from you very soon.

Sincerely,

7. Solicit an out-of-town property owner (Figure 6–9).

FIGURE 6–9
Soliciting an Out-of-Town Owner

Dear

When reviewing the property tax records, I noted that you owned the property at _____.

Every year many "out-of-city" owners decide to sell or trade their real estate holdings. In our continuing effort to better serve owners of property in this community, I am taking this opportunity to offer our services in the sale of your _____ real estate.

The sale of your property can be handled in several ways:

1. A direct all-cash sale.
2. A direct part-cash sale, with you carrying the mortgage.
3. An immediate cash purchase of your property by our company, for resale at our convenience.
4. A trade for other local property. (This is an excellent method to establish a new depreciation schedule for tax shelter purposes.)

The _____ real estate market is holding at a steady level, with most sellers getting their price.

If you are interested in selling your property, please let me know. I will start to work immediately on a thorough study and appraisal. When these are finished, I will send you a complete analysis of your property and our listing form.

Sincerely,

8. Get a change of terms or price (Figure 6–10).

FIGURE 6–10
Suggesting a Change of Price or Terms

Dear

I am concerned that we have not yet produced an acceptable sales contract on your home. Statistically, a home like yours should sell within 43 days. We have been working on your property 41 days.

As we discussed, Mr. _____, 65 percent of the buying public in _____ are veterans. By not advertising that we will consider selling to veterans, we are ignoring 65 out of every 100 buyers. And frankly, there are now just not that many buyers.

Not only are we confronted with a lack of available financing for conventional buyers, but also, as last Sunday's newspaper pointed out, the busing problem is depressing the _____ market, especially in your neighborhood.

I strongly urge you to sell on VA terms. If you agree, please mail me a check for $50 payable to _____ Mortgage Company, and I will order a VA appraisal for you.

Remember the four elements necessary for every successful sale: price, terms, condition, and salesmanship.

Even if I were not an effective salesman, your home has been shown by many other _____ salespersons besides me, as well as other brokers who have shared the listing in Multi-List.

I believe that the condition and the location of your property are good. The price, I believe, is certainly within a range of what it should sell for.

Therefore, we should try adjusting the terms.

With kindest regards,

---

9. Follow up an interview for a potential listing (Figure 6–11).

FIGURE 6–11
Following Up an Interview for a Potential Listing

Dear

Thank you for taking the time to show me your beautiful home. I was quite surprised to discover how large and how nice it is.

When it is convenient for you, let me know, and I will be pleased to meet with you and your husband to discuss the marketing of your house.

With regard to the time element, I would like to point out that in this southeast area it takes an average of 71 days from the time a house is listed until it is sold. It takes another four to six weeks after that before the sale is "closed."

It is to your advantage to place your house on the market just as quickly as possible. You want to give yourself ample time and not have to be cornered into accepting a low offer.

The present market conditions are in your favor. At this moment very few desirable houses are on the market in our area. Therefore, you are not competing with other sales, and the demand for our neighborhood is high.

You need not worry about being "thrown out into the street," since you merely stipulate that possession not be given until a certain date.

I look forward to assisting you.

Sincerely,

10. Confirm a price reduction or a change of terms (Figure 6–12).

FIGURE 6–12
Confirming a Change of Terms

Dear

This letter confirms our conversation of _____, in which you agreed to reduce the price of your property at _____ for the period from _____ to _____.

Our staff has been advised of this change and will exert every possible effort to bring you a satisfactory contract at an early date.

Yours truly,

---

11. Announce that a particular salesperson will be farming a certain area (Figure 6–13).

FIGURE 6–13
Paving the Way for Farming an Area

Dear

For some time now, we have been searching for a salesperson to represent the _____ area. Now I'm delighted to announce the choice has been made.

_____ will call on you within the next couple of months to introduce himself. Of all the sales associates in our _____ office, _____ was our unanimous choice. He's a warm, intelligent, experienced man with a splendid sales and service background. His experience includes _____ and over _____ years of sales experience with our company. He's a man in whom you can put your confidence.

When Mr. _____ comes by, I hope you'll have the time to talk to him. Then you'll see why we have placed our complete confidence in him. However, if you have an immediate need for real estate counseling, please call him.

Sincerely,

---

12. Convince renters of the value of buying real estate (Figure 6–14).

FIGURE 6–14
Approaching Renters

2768 south wadsworth boulevard · denver, colorado 80227 · 303/989-1870

RENTS ARE GOING UP!!! The rents are going up and the interest rates
on home loans are down. There has never been a better time to buy
a home. Invest your money in a home where you can build an equity
for future investment.

Compare the Actual Monthly Cost on the enclosed analysis sheet with
the rent you are paying now. So why are you renting? Have you considered purchasing a home?

The benefits of buying a home are numerous in comparison to the pitfalls of throwing your hard earned money away on rent. You should
have the privilege of building an equity, and the privacy that you
are entitled to.

Call or mail in the card today. I will be glad to discuss with you
any questions you have in regard to purchasing a home or investment
opportunities in Real Estate.

Sincerely,

MEMBER OF THE NATIONAL ASSOCIATION OF REALTORS   REALTOR®

FIGURE 6–14 (*continued*)

2768 /outh wad/worth boulevard · denver. colorado 80227 · 303/989-1870

Sale Price of Home . . . . $ 35,000.00

    Cash . . . . $ 1,400.00 plus closing costs

    Loan . . . . $ 33,600.00   30   years, at   8.5 %

Monthly Payment: Principal and Interest. . . . . $ 259.00

Monthly Deposit: Taxes (approximately) . . . . . $ 41.00

Monthly Deposit: Insurance (approximately) . . . $ 10.00

             TOTAL MONTHLY PAYMENT. . . . . $ 310.00

Expense Items for Income Tax Purposes:

    First month interest. . . . . . $ 238.00

    Monthly tax deposit . . . . . . $ 41.00

          TOTAL. . . . . $ 279.00

If buyer is in 50% tax bracket, deduct $_____(50% of sum deposit
                      and tax deposit)
If buyer is in 40% tax bracket, deduct $_____(40% of sum deposit
                      and tax deposit)
If buyer is in 30% tax bracket, deduct $ 84.00 (30% of sum deposit
                      and tax deposit)

Total monthly payment. . . . . $ 310.00

Less: Deduction. . . . . $ 84.00   -   30 %bracket

Real monthly payment . . . . $ 226.00

    EQUITY WHICH IS BEING GAINED MONTHLY . .   7   % - $ 204.00

    Real monthly payment. . . . . $ 226.00

    Less: Equity gained . . . . . $ 204.00

    ACTUAL MONTHLY COST . . . . . $ 22.00

(The monthly credit against taxable income decreases a few cents monthly,
but the equity increases by the same amount. This form applies to
taxpayer who uses itemized deductions.)

050/7/76

13. Provide a monthly newsletter for one's farm (geographic or associational) (Figure 6–15).

FIGURE 6–15
A Monthly Farm Letter

REAL ESTATE BRIEFS

From the desk of JOHN F. VANNEMAN
March/April

HOME PRICES UP FASTEST IN THREE YEARS

The average price of new homes last year went up at the fastest pace in three years, the government reported last week.

The Commerce Department said the average price of new single family homes sold last year was $48,000, up 12.7 per cent from the $42,600 the previous year. Prices had climbed 9.5 per cent in 1975. Last year's increase was the sharpest since the 16.4 per cent increase in 1973.

Predictions for the future unfortunately for those considering buying in the future are for prices to continue to rise drastically. If you are thinking of buying or trading your home for a larger one, now is probably the best time to do so.

TWO THOUSAND CHEESMAN EAST

Moore and Company has been named the exclusive sales representative for an exciting high rise condominium complex at 1200 Race Street named Two-Thousand Cheesman East.

Cheesman East is made up of 26 floors of luxury condominiums of which there are no more than 3 units per floor. Buyers can choose from the 1408 square feet, 2 bedroom unit which ranges in price from $75,000 to $96,000 on up to the 2816 square feet, 3 bedroom which is two-thirds of a floor and costs up to about $192,000. (Quite an elaborate layout is this one.)

All of the higher units have magnificent views of the mountains from Longs Peak on the North, Southward to Pikes Peak near Colorado Springs. You also are overlooking Cheesman Park and the Botanic Gardens just out over your lanai.

Other amenities of Two-Thousand Cheesman East include an indoor swimming pool, aspen sauna, and steam room. For the handball, racquett ball, and tennis enthusiast there are two indoor courts as well as two individual outdoor tennis courts. It is like having your own health club right at home.

You are all cordially invited to visit Two-Thousand Cheesman East on your next visit downtown.

Moore and company
REALTOR

FIGURE 6-15 (*continued*)

FOR SALE

In response to my Jan/Feb newsletter I do have a few items that my readers have asked me to advertise. Any of you that might be interested in seeing any of these items can call these people advertising their items for sale direct.

FOR SALE: Only $50.00 for a <u>Sea Snark</u> sail boat. Be a fun boat for sailing in Washington Park or Cherry Creek. Call Peggy McKay 733-4376.

FOR SALE: <u>Howard Lorton Sofa</u>, 90" soft flame velvet, tufted back, individually zippered cushions, $600.00. Call Virginia Nielson 935-0072.

FOR SALE: Brand new, never been installed or used <u>Hot Point Electric Range</u>. Pink color, only $100.00. Call Virginia Nielson 935-0072.

FOR SALE: <u>1965 Volkswagen Baja Buggy</u>. 1969 engine, sun roof, mechanically sound but needs some work. $400.00 call Jon McConkey 744-9530.

FOR SALE: This is a masterpiece and must be seen. Lighted <u>Colorado Mountain Scene Panarama</u>. Includes 2 lions, 4 mountain sheep and numerous trees and rock formations. All to 1/10th life size. Professionally hand made by Lester F. Carlson who was formerly with Jonas Brothers Taxidermy for 32 years. Call 934-2630.

For those of you advertising I hope this ad will attract some buyers. Anyone interested in advertising an item in my next issue, please call me around the middle of April for my May/June newsletter.

TAX NOTE

For those of you that have family or friends that are considering selling their homes here, some good news from congress if they are over 65 years of age. There will be no capital gain tax from the sale of the property on a gain now up to $35,000. This became effective December 31, 1976. Previously only $20,000 of the gain was tax exempt for our senior citizens, but now they can save an extra $15,000 of their tax burden. Feel free to call me if I can provide you with any additional information on this subject.

Hope that you have enjoyed and gained some information from my newsletter.

Best regards,

John F Vanneman.

John F. Vanneman

Doing business... **Moore Way**

FORM R-10 — 5/76 CROWN

14. Canvass an area for a particular type of property (Figure 6–16).

FIGURE 6–16
Canvassing for a Buyer

Dear

    I have a client who is interested in a home in your area.
He and his wife have _____ children, ages _____ through
_____. They are interested in purchasing a home which most nearly
fits the following description:

    In the event that you are considering selling in the near future, or
that you know anyone in your area who is considering the sale of such
a home, I would be most grateful if you would contact me.

                    Sincerely,

THE TELEPHONE

According to Murray Roman, chairman of Champaign Communications Institute of America, Inc., in his book *Telephone Marketing* (New York: McGraw-Hill Book Co., 1976), "Before the lights go out tonight in United States households from Maine to Hawaii, some 7 million Americans will answer their phones, while someone they've never seen or heard of tries to sell them something . . . and fully 460,000 will buy what is being offered." (p. 1)

The telephone is an indispensable tool in any effective sales program. The instrument can be used:

1. To service present clients.
2. To maintain contact with former clients.
3. To cold-prospect for new clients.
4. To solicit referrals.

In the total sales campaign, the phone can be used as a preapproach instrument (to set appointments) or as a follow-up medium (after an introduction by letter).

Thus, in using the telephone the real estate salesperson must first establish the answer to the questions:

Why do you call?

As an example of the use of the telephone as a follow-up medium, Don Galemba, $4 million producer of Van Schaack & Company of Colorado, explains that he first mails a letter and accompanying material and then phones several days later.

In pursuing FSBOs, for instance, Don's introductory letter might enclose a "moving checklist" (that is, things to do when moving out of an old home or into a new home); a blank receipt and option contract showing what things FSBOs will need to consider when an offer is brought to them; some tax information relative to the sale of a personal residence, or a brochure that the FSBOs could complete and distribute as a handout.

Within a week, Don follows up with a phone call inquiring whether the homeowners received the material, whether they found it useful, and whether there is something else they would like to have. From that point on, he talks toward arranging a time when he can stop by on an appointment basis to see the home and meet with the people.

Don does not feel that he is imposing on the homeowners or approaching them at a bad time. "I feel that puts me in a better position than someone who just goes up to a door and knocks on it cold."

Jim Spurling, broker associate of Moore Realty, Colorado, identifies some of the values of the phone as a prospecting instrument.

He points out that in face-to-face canvassing you would be fortunate if 8 out of 15 owners were at home. Thus "you have wasted your time in trying to contact the remaining seven. In their case, you haven't talked to anybody. So you have lost the main advantage of a face-to-face meeting, unless you make an attempt to go back and see them at a later time. But then you are doubling your expenditure of effort. On the other hand, it only takes ten seconds to determine by phone whether anyone is home.

"Also, if you should try to go out and it begins to snow or rain hard, you have lost a day or more. But you can phone in all kinds of weather."

Whom do you call?

Having determined *why* he or she is phoning, the salesperson must answer the question *Whom do you call?*

If you are prospecting for new clients, it is preferable to select some homogeneous grouping. Will that grouping consist of income property owners or resident homeowners? If you decide to canvass income property owners, will they be owners of small units (duplexes, triplexes) or of larger apartments? If you should decide to obtain single-family residences, will you make your calls according to the prices of homes, the types of homes, or the location of homes?

Once you have determined your market, the sources of information noted in Chapters 2 and 4 (Polk's *City Directory*, Cole's *Directory*, and the REDI volumes) can be used to define whom to phone.

When do you call?

Equally important is your answer to the question *When do you call?* The times of the day and the days of the week must be determined according to local custom, the reason for the call, and the persons being called. For instance, it is inappropriate to call some people on Saturdays (for example, Orthodox Jews) and other people on Sunday mornings.

What do you say?

As Murray Roman counsels in discussing *script presentation,* "Although you know exactly how effective a salesperson you are, it should be stressed once again that the techniques required for telephone salesmanship differ materially from those you may have very successfully employed during face-to-face-selling." (p. 106)

The differences include the need to answer immediately and without hesitation. Work out a series of questions that you expect to be asked and the answers that you will give. In the beginning, have these questions and answers close at hand while you phone.

"Because the person you have called cannot see you, it is not feasible to try to open your contact call with the same personalized techniques that many salespeople have learned to use with such great success in their personal calls. No comments about the weather . . . no jokes about golf." (p. 108)

It is essential, instead, to get to the point immediately and briefly.

Any script, Rowan explains, should always follow this format:

1. Ask for the prospect by name, and verify that he or she is the person on the phone.
2. Announce the name of the caller.
3. Identify the name of the organization the caller represents.
4. State the general nature of the call.

"By following these four proved steps, you can obtain your prospect's undivided attention in a matter of about 20 seconds." (p. 47)

A presentation that many listors use with FSBOs is similar to the following. After the owners' names have been obtained from the source materials discussed earlier, the listor dials the number.

1. "Hello. May I speak with Mr. or Mrs. X, please? [*The called party will then answer.*] Mr. X? . . . Are you the party with the house for sale? ("Yes.")
2. "This is _____ with _____ Realty Company. [*Without stopping, ask:*]
3. "Would you be kind enough to give me some information about your house?"

At this point expect: "We don't want to list with a real estate broker." *To this you may reply,* "I realize that. But I saw your advertisement [*or sign*], and I need to keep abreast of properties for my clients." *Then, without stopping, ask:*

4. "How much are you asking?" [*Or,* "Is it correct that you are asking $_____?"]
5. "For what reason are you selling your home?"
6. "If I sold your house for $_____ [*the price they have set on their house*], would you pay a commission?"
7. (*If the answer is no:*) "If I brought you a contract for $_____ [*their price*] *plus* my commission, would this be acceptable?
8. "May I see your home at [*time*] today?"

How do you say it?

The question *How do you say it?* requires the real estate salesperson to realize that he or she should:

1. "Dial with a smile." Tests have shown unequivocally that you cannot conceal your attitude and feelings over the phone. If for any reason you are feeling "out of sorts," put off phoning until your condition improves.

2. Speak distinctly, and adjust the speed of your delivery to what you sense is your listener's mood. You might try tape-recording one of your telephone conversations. Then, play back the tape, analyze the speed and diction of your conversation, and make the appropriate corrections.

3. Keep your statements and questions brief, and allow the listener to respond so that you engage in a conversation rather than a monologue.

4. Be courteous, regardless of the other person's response.

5. Be persistent. Prospecting by phone has been described as a "numbers game." Don't give up.

Most of the top listors are convinced of the value of using the phone in their sales program. Yet, figures of conversion success are difficult to obtain, since it seems that usually the more successful the producer, the less time he or she has for detailed record keeping. In other words, the successful producers know that using the telephone works and therefore see no reason to keep records that prove it works.

Off and on, Bruce Jorgensen tries to keep some sort of score. Out of 20 numbers dialed in his latest study, he was able to make contact with 10 owners. One of the owners requested and was furnished with a market analysis; one said that he would retire and relocate in 1982; one was moving to Black Duck in 1978; and one was retiring in 1978.

Jorgensen evaluates this as one immediate prospect and three long-term prospects. Since real estate is his career, a lead five years away is still a lead.

Chuck Cooper, sales associate of Carolyn Rosen Riteway, Miami, Florida, relies heavily upon phone solicitation in his sales program. Chuck works 1 to 1½ hours at a stretch of serious phoning. He averages about ten calls per hour. And out of that "I can get three or four promising leads." He follows up each phone contact with a thank-you card.

His phone message is brief. "This is Chuck Cooper of Carolyn Rosen Riteway. I notice from the tax rolls that you are the owner of _____, and I've called to ask if you have ever considered selling?" (If not: "Do you know of anyone in your neighborhood who is?")

Since many persons seem to be fearful about taking advantage of the phone, Jim Spurling advises, "To overcome anything, you have to do it. In other words, the more you do something, the more comfortable you get. It's just like people playing golf for the first time. They look like an elephant with arthritis—awkward as can be. They don't know what to do. What the moves are.

"The same way with working the phone. The first time you are hit with an objection, you say, 'Oh, I'm sorry. Ah . . . thank you very much.' Click. And you are off the phone.

"But then you sit and think about it. 'OK, now what's the logical answer to that objection?' You may even find yourself writing the answer down. The next time the objection comes up, you handle it a little better. Then by the time you have worked with the phone hundreds of times, there's hardly anything an owner can throw at you that you haven't heard before.

"By doing it, you chip away the rough edges."

Like other listors who use the phone extensively and effectively, Jim does not concern himself with statistics. In addition to noting that the better salespersons probably neither have the time nor the inclination to maintain copious figures (otherwise they'd probably be in accounting), Jim points out that the reliability of such statistics would be highly questionable because of variations in (1) the approach, (2) the personalities of the individuals who use a given approach, and (3) the groups to which the approach is directed.

"The personality variations alone would seriously affect the true picture."

Nevertheless, he regards the telephone as an effective device within the total listing program.

Don Weaver of Jim Owen Realty, Columbus, Ohio, a multi-million-dollar producer and a top listor, is always on the move. Consequently, he considers the recorded message operating on his residence phone to be of vital importance to him.

"Hi. This is Don Weaver. Sorry I am out at the moment, but if you will answer the following questions, I will return your call.

"What is you phone number? [*Pause for caller to reply*]

"What is your name? [*Pause*]

"Which newpaper ad or property address are you calling about? [*Pause*]

"Do you have any other questions? [*Pause*]

"Thank you."

ADVERTISING

We are limiting our account of the listing pros' reviews on the uses of newspaper advertising to those that have already been cited in this book, mainly because so much has been written in this field and because newspaper advertising is largely company or management controlled.

Most of the top listors caution the real estate salesperson against becoming a junk merchant as regards handouts. The selection criteria of the top listors are that the item given (1) should be useful, (2) should show the giver's name prominently, and (3) should be consumable, so that the user will want a replacement.

Scratch pads similar to those Don Nourse leaves with occupants in his farm area are considered ideal by many listors. Don's pads measure 3 inches $\times$ 8 inches (other listors use 4-inch $\times$ 5-inch pads) and have 50 sheets. At the bottom of each sheet are the words "Don Nourse, Your Turtle Rock Specialist," along with Don's phone number. When Don goes door to door in his farm, he puts the pad in a plastic bag that he hangs from the doorknob whenever the occupant is not at home. The reception is excellent.

Along with other customary gifts, John Vanneman of Moore Realty of Colorado provides his buyers with a subscription to *Colorado Magazine* beginning the month they occupy their new home.

7

The Presentation

The listing picture is a mosaic which includes prospecting for sellers; accumulating, preparing, and packaging appropriate information; and making the listing presentation.

As noted earlier, prospective sellers can be located by such methods as canvassing, contacting FSBOs, developing a locational or an associational farm, and nurturing repeat business and referrals.

EFFECTIVE PROSPECTING QUESTIONS

Typically, in searching for prospects the real estate salesperson is inclined to rely upon the question "Do you know anybody who is thinking of buying or selling real estate?"

And when he keeps hearing the answer "No," the average salesperson becomes discouraged. He begins to worry about whether he offends others by asking such a question. "What's the matter?" he wonders.

In developing the best methods, many top listors have discovered the advantage of studying and using the methods of salespeople in other occupations. Many real estate salespeople have borrowed, for example, some of the techniques of the insurance industry. And one of the most difficult forms of selling is life insurance.

The life insurance industry learned long ago to caution its agents against asking "Do you know anyone who wants to buy life insurance?" Almost naturally, the answer will be "No." And for at least two reasons. First, despite the need for life insurance, no one seems to *want* to buy life insurance except persons who are uninsurable because of a terminal health condition.

Second, most people do not know enough about the affairs of others to recognize who wants or needs life insurance. Hence, the life insurance agent is taught how to assess what conditions in a person's life frequently warrant the purchase of life insurance. Accordingly, he asks those questions which will identify for him those people who have experienced or who are about to experience certain changes in their life-styles.

A similar situation exists for the real estate listor. To begin with, the need to sell a house often arises suddenly, for example, because of a company transfer. Very often, therefore, the prospective seller is himself unaware until the last minute that he "wants to sell any real estate."

If the question "Do you know anyone who is thinking of buying or selling real estate?" had been asked of such a transferee a few minutes before his notice was given him, he too would have answered "No."

Even when sellers are contemplating a move, they do not always share their intention of selling with others until they have formulated their plans. In such cases, then, friends or neighbors would not necessarily know about the anticipated sale.

If the real estate salesperson would stop and meditate upon this issue, he would soon realize that the odds are that this typical question will be answered with a "No" even by those persons who are most anxious to help the listor.

The point, obviously, is that the real estate salesperson must rephrase his questioning. He must ask questions which will identify for him people who are undergoing changes or are about to undergo changes. It will then be up to the salesperson to assess the circumstances and the nature of the changes to determine whether or not he has located a prospective seller.

For example, assume that you ask someone very close to you for a lead. Let's say that it is your mother, to emphasize the point.

"Mom. Do you know anyone who is thinking of buying or selling real estate?"

"Oh, I wish I could help you. But . . . no . . . I can't think of a single soul."

But, instead, suppose that you asked your mother: "Mom, do any of your friends have big families?"

"Well, of course," she answers quizzically.

"Which ones do you know whose last child is going away to college, or off to the service, or getting married?"

"Well, let's see," she ponders. "There are the Blimps . . . I don't think you've ever met them. I met Helen Blimp . . . oh, I can't remember. But anyway, I think she told me they raised four or five children. They live in a big two-story house over in Park View. Our circle met there once . . . about two months ago. In fact, I met Helen's youngest child then, a girl. She's getting married . . . come to think of it . . . I believe she said . . . in April . . . Yes, I know it's April because after the wedding Helen and her husband are going on that Ports-of-Call trip with us all the 17th of April. And then, when they come back, they are thinking of buying one of those town houses over in Thickwood. You know . . . come to think of it . . . maybe you ought to talk to them."

You bet you should! You have a prospect.

No longer, therefore, should you ask, "Do you know anybody who is thinking of buying or selling real estate?"

Instead, develop the habit of formulating your questions along the lines of these samples:

1. Do you know anyone who has recently been promoted?
2. Do you know anyone who is about to be or has recently been transferred?
3. Do you know anyone whose child is about to be or has recently been graduated?
4. Do you know anyone who has recently been or is about to be retired?
5. Do you know anyone who has recently been or is about to be married?
6. Do you know anyone who is about to be divorced?
7. Do you know anyone who has recently purchased a Winnebago?
8. Do you know anyone who has recently been fired from his job?
9. Do you know anyone who has recently received an inheritance?
10. Do you know who is "fixing up" his property?

THE SELLER'S DILEMMA

Regardless of the source of a listing lead—canvassing, referral, and so forth—the listor must realize that *every* seller progresses through the steps of resolving in his own mind whether he needs a real estate broker, why he needs a particular broker, why he should select a particular listor, and what price he can obtain for his property.

Most sellers find it difficult to answer these questions. One reason is that they are so infrequently involved in the buying and selling of real estate. Professor Frederick E. Case notes that "because of this infrequent market participation . . . sellers have little basis for judging one real estate office as compared with another; therefore, they are likely to be completely capricious in the selection of an office to handle their transactions.

"Because of the general lack of knowledge of . . . sellers with respect to the complexities of real estate property transfers, and because of the requirement that they pay a percentage of the purchase price for the services of someone who apparently does nothing but insert a small advertisement in the paper, they are easy prey for unscrupulous dealers who promise them almost anything in order to handle their transaction. These assumptions may even encourage . . . sellers to attempt to complete their transactions without the services of a real estate broker."[1]

WHY A REAL ESTATE BROKER?

To establish the need for using a real estate broker, the listor discusses one or more of the following functions of real estate brokers.

1. Arrange Financing. Buyers need not be turned away because they do not have cash. The competent real estate broker is expert in advising which of many ways are best for financing a transaction. These include the following:

a. Assumption of existing loan.
b. Collateral loans (with the seller providing additional security to the lender to increase the loan amount).
c. Contract for deed (or an installment land contract whereby title does not pass until all or most of the amount is paid).
d. Conventional financing (loans of 60 percent to 95 percent, with

---

1 *Real Estate Brokerage,* Prentice-Hall, Inc., Englewood Cliffs, N.J., 1965, p. 254.

and without accompanying private mortgage insurance, from savings and loans, mortgage bankers and brokers, insurance companies, credit unions, and so on).

e. Equity advance (a temporary loan equal to the equity in the seller's existing property).
f. Exchange.
g. FHA-insured Loan.
h. FmHA (Farmers Home Administration guaranteed or direct loans).
i. Purchase money mortgage (with the owner financing the first mortgage).
j. Second mortgage (with varying repayment combinations).
k. VA-guaranteed loans.
l. Wraparound mortgage (with the one periodic financing payment including the amount of the original mortgage payment).

The competent real estate broker keeps in constant touch with lenders to ascertain:

a. Who is in charge of lending.
b. Who should be contacted.
c. What type of money is currently available.
d. The current interest rates.
e. The current discount points.
f. What insurance is required.
g. Which lenders will accept second-mortgage and collateral deposit financing.
h. When loan committees meet.
i. Their standard turnaround time on closings.
j. And so forth.

2. Assist in Avoiding Legal Entanglements. In most states the real estate broker is permitted to make out the legal documents required to complete the real estate transaction. With the real estate broker's professional guidance, the seller is freed from red tape and possible litigation. In those states which restrict or prohibit the real estate broker from making out and explaining the contract and its legal effects, the real estate broker can refer the seller to a competent *real estate* attorney.

3. Qualify the Buyer. The skillful real estate broker will sift "lookers" from buyers and eliminate unqualified shoppers. When a buyer phones the owner direct to obtain the price and the address, or when a prospect drives by the property, the sale may be lost because of the manner in which the seller answers the caller's questions or because of the exterior condition of the property. The real estate broker objectively assesses what the buyer wants, and knows how to handle objections relative to price, location, and condition. Real estate brokers match buyers with properties and steer buyers to the properties they want.

4. Negotiate on Behalf of the Seller. If the buyer asks, "Will you take less?" and the seller answers "Yes," the buyer more than likely will persist on "How much less?" The seller is confronted with the dilemma of holding on to the buyer yet not losing his equity. An experienced negotiator can salvage both, as well as protect the seller from investment speculators.

5. Regulate Showings. In this way the real estate salesperson can minimize disruption of the seller's home life. When selling his own home, the homeowner feels compelled to open it for inspection whenever a buyer asks to see it. In addition, the seller is confined to his home until the property is sold. If he leaves his home, he is, in effect, taking it "off the market."

6. Aid in Securing the Safety of the Seller's Family. Since the real estate salesperson is present at all showings, the seller's family need not be fearful of showing the home to strangers whose motives they cannot question.

7. Formulate the Best Marketing Program. Erecting a sign and running an ad are only portions of an effective marketing program. Only the real estate salesperson has the expertise and the tools with which to effectively merchandise real property.

8. Properly Price the Property. Most sellers do not have the education, knowledge, experience, or tools to arrive at a fair market value of their property. The real estate broker is equipped to protect both the seller and the buyer. Many buyers are reluctant to deal directly with a seller because they do not know how to buy a house and because they cannot be certain that the price they pay is equitable. The reputable real estate broker is obliged by ethics and by sound business practices to be certain that neither his client nor the buyer is defrauded.

Listors with Laguarta, Gavrel and Kirk, Inc., explain to clients that "when a house is sold *someone* always gets the commission: the real estate company or agent, the buyer, or the seller." When a homeowner attempts to sell his own property, according to Laguarta, Gavrel & Kirk, Inc., the *buyer* always has the advantage because:

1. He has experience in comparing many homes.
2. He has guidance, help, and protection from his lawyer, his bank, and the like.
3. He can quickly estimate a bargain price and substract the commission, and in that way give the commisssion to himself.
4. He sets the terms of the contract (if there is one).
5. He has the ability to make the seller come to him.
6. He knows that the seller is not being advised by a real estate broker.
7. He has hundreds of homes to choose from, whereas the seller has only one home to sell.
8. Although the seller and his family know nothing about the buyer, they must show him through the home at any time.
9. Unless the seller's home is a real bargain, the seller needs the buyer more than the buyer needs the seller.
10. He may tie up the seller's home with a verbal offer, then never return, causing the seller to pass up other prospective buyers.
11. He will buy, for the most part, only if he can steal a piece of property.

A real estate broker can obtain fair market value for the seller, which is what the seller is looking for.

"You might think you would save money by dealing directly with a purchaser, but there is a strong possibility that with your lack of training, knowledge, and experience, you might get stung. We can ask pertinent questions which you are unable to ask concerning a purchaser's financial capabilities to buy.

"There is just one real reason a buyer answers a 'For Sale by Owner' ad—MONEY. The money he intends to save, at your expense.

"Yes—someone will get a commission on the sale of your home. If the buyer gets it, he gets *your* time, aggravation, and work, and worry —free! Plus whatever he can bargain off the net price. If Laguarta, Gavrel & Kirk, Inc., REALTORS®, get it, you get complete, professional service, and it costs you nothing extra."

WHY THIS REAL ESTATE BROKER?

If the seller becomes convinced that he needs a real estate broker, he must then decide which real estate broker to employ.

Don Nourse's comments to a prospective seller illustrate the types of remarks a real estate broker may make:

"Most brokers are capable of providing you with signs, advertising, an open house, brochures, local prospects, local broker participation, a direct mail campaign, negotiating on your behalf, and some outside relocation service.

"But in addition to providing you with the services other brokers can provide, Coldwell Banker is the largest diversified real estate company in the United States. Our company has sold real estate for 70 years. None of our 3,900 employees is a part-timer. With 183 offices, we have 183 ways to sell your home and a national relocation network. Better than 66 percent of our customers come to us.

"We know how to price your home from two points of view: to be sold and to be bought. In that way, it's not a one-sided thing. And we provide a total range of real estate services. We are listed on the New York Stock Exchange. We have a national image, longevity, management depth, financial strength, and specially trained personnel. Our constant, ongoing, up-to-date training programs make our salespeople experts in real estate."

THE PRIME CHARACTERISTICS OF A
SUCCESSFUL LISTOR

One reason sellers find it difficult to choose a real estate broker is that they are confronted by so many "salespeople" who really do not know what they are doing or how to assist the sellers.

Says Dave McGinnis, "My approach is no different from that of other successful brokers, and that is just catching the sellers off guard. They are not used to being confronted by professionals."

"You have to set yourself off as being a little bit different from or a little bit better than the general horde," adds Charles Howe.

(See Figures 7–1, 7–2, and 7–3 for examples of one broker's attempt to distinguish his firm.)

According to Loretta Baginski, a leading listor for Laguarta, Gavrel & Kirk, Inc., Houston, "If you are prepared, make a good appearance and a good presentation, and know what you are talking about, there is no reason for not getting the listing. But a listor must know what he is talking about."

Ray Novotny points out rather emphatically, "There is a euphemism going around. They call it 'being professional.' Which means to put on a nice suit of clothes and get all dressed up and make a listing presentation. But the trouble is that often when sellers start asking

FIGURE 7-1
A Listing Warranty

2768 south wadsworth boulevard · denver, colorado 80227 · 303 989-1870

LISTING WARRANTY

In order to provide our clients with a service that is "a little bit better" and "a little bit different", GEORGE REALTY COMPANY is executing this "Listing Warranty" concurrently with our Exclusive Right To Sell Listing Contract. GEORGE REALTY COMPANY agrees to perform the following services for you, the seller, on your property at

1. Provide a Comparative Market Analysis of your property based on available market data.

2. Review with you the GEORGE REALTY COMPANY list of twenty ways to "Let Your Home Smile A Welcome To Folks Who Want To Buy".

3. Review with you the five major methods of real estate financing including F.H.A. and V.A. discount "points".

4. Submit pertinent data regarding your home to Multiple Listing Service within *five* business days for printing the special picture brochure and publication in the M.L.S. book.

5. Distribute picture brochures regarding your property to other brokers in the area and at M.L.S. meetings.

6. Have the GEORGE REALTY COMPANY'S sales "team" preview or "caravan" your property within seven business days.

7. Erect a unique GEORGE REALTY COMPANY yard sign on your property within 48 hours.

8. Conduct an effective advertising program to "expose" your property to as many prospective buyers as possible.

9. Pre-qualify buyers and show your property by appointment only, to eliminate unnecessary inconvenience to you.

10. Provide a status report four times a month, either by telephone or personal visit, as to your property's progress toward a sale until sold.

This agreement is made with the understanding that the ten above described services will be performed by GEORGE REALTY COMPANY and its sales associates to your complete satisifaction. If such is not the case, the Exclusive Right To Sell Listing Contract will be cancelled at any time during the listing period, upon the undersigned having received written notice of reason of dissatisfaction from you.

GEORGE REALTY COMPANY

_____   _____
President   Date

028/10/76

FIGURE 7–2
A Discussion of Points

2768 south wadsworth boulevard · denver, colorado 80227 · 303/989-1870

MORTGAGE DISCOUNT POINTS

1. **WHAT ARE MORTGAGE DISCOUNT POINTS?**

    A mortgage is "discounted" when it sells for less than its principal amount.

    EXAMPLE:
    ```
    Principal amount of mortgage . . . . . . . 30,000
          Sold For. . . . . . . . . . . . . . . 29,100
    DISCOUNT . . . . . . . . . . . . . . . .      900
    ```

    Thus the mortgage discount is $900 or 3%.

    The 3% is called <u>three</u> "<u>Points</u>".

2. **WHY DO WE HAVE DISCOUNT POINTS?**

    Interest may be defined as the wages for money.

    The Federal Government regulates the current rate on FHA and GI loans at 8½% interest.

    This rate is <u>less</u> than the market interest rates on conventional loans and other investments.

    Since FHA and GI loans earn less interest the <u>only way</u> they can be made "equally productive" is by collecting Discount Points.

3. **WHO DETERMINES THE AMOUNT OF DISCOUNT POINTS?**

    Generally speaking no one person or organization regulates the amount of Discount Points.

    Money for loans is a commodity in the market. As a commodity it is subject to the law of supply and demand.

    A so-called "tight money" situation is created when the <u>demand</u> <u>exceeds</u> the <u>supply</u>. In this kind of market the discount may increase to 6 or 8 points.

    When the opposite occurs and the <u>supply exceeds</u> the <u>demand</u>, the discount may decrease to 2 or 3 points.

FIGURE 7-2 (*continued*)

MORTGAGE DISCOUNT POINTS (CONT.)

4. WHO PAYS THE DISCOUNT POINTS?

The seller or builder pays the discount points when a new
FHA or GI loan is secured.

5. WHO PROFITS MOST FROM DISCOUNT POINTS?

The seller of the property usually receives the most benefit.

Most buyers will pay a slightly higher price for your property if they can purchase it with a Minimum Down Payment
FHA Loan; or No Down Payment GI Loan.

For this reason, you, the seller, receive a fair price for
your property in Cash.

The Realty Company or Salesman does not receive any of the
Discount Points.

6. WHY SHOULD THE SELLER PAY THE DISCOUNT POINTS?

The buyer is prohibited by Federal Law from paying the discount points. Since "points" are used to raise the effective
interest rate on the loan, the buyer would be paying a
higher interest than the law allows.

The seller is able to attract more buyers, and "Cash Out, by
offering FHA or GI financing to the new buyer.

7. WHO RECEIVES THE DISCOUNT POINTS?

The bank or lender receives the discount points.

8. WHEN ARE THE DISCOUNT POINTS PAID?

At the time the new new loan is made by the lender.

9. CAN WE AVOID PAYING DISCOUNT POINTS?

Yes, by requiring your buyer to pay Cash for your equity
or secure a conventional loan. However, this would probably cost you more than you could save on the Discount
Points.

By eliminating all FHA and GI buyers for your house, the
final selling price would problably be less than the
discount points you are asked to pay.

Conventional lenders generally lend 70% to 90% of the Sales
Price on residential property. So, your buyer would need
a 10% to 30% Cash Down Payment or you, as the Seller, would
be asked to carry a sizeable Second Deed of Trust.

GEORGE REALTY CO./ 2768 /outh wad/worth boulevard · denver, colorado 80227 · 303 989-1870

042/10/76

FIGURE 7–3
Showing Instructions

2768 south wadsworth boulevard · denver. colorado 80227 · 303/989-1870

LET YOUR HOME SMILE A WELCOME TO
FOLKS WHO WANT TO BUY

We have your home for sale because you want to sell it. With little effort on your part, this can be accomplished more quickly and at a better price. Arouse the prospect's desire for your home by making it attractive. Here are twenty tested tips to help us show your home to its best advantage. One of them may be applicable to you or your home. We find our efforts are most successful when the stage is well set.

PREPARATION FOR SHOWING

1. First impressions are lasting impressions. An inviting exterior insures inspection of the interior. Keep your lawn trimmed and edged - flower beds cultivated - the yard free and clear of refuse.

2. Decorate your home - a step toward a SALE. Faded walls and woodwork that looks worn reduce "desire." Do not tell the prospect how the place can be made to look - show him by decorating first. A quicker sale at a higher price will result.

3. Cleanliness is next to Godliness. Bright, cheery windows and unmarred walls will assist your sales.

4. Fix that faucet. Dripping water discolors the enamel and calls attention to faulty plumbing.

5. A day with the carpenter. Loose door knobs, sticking drawers, warped cabinet doors and the like are noticed by the prospect. Have them fixed.

6. From top to bottom. The attic and basement are important features. All unnecessary articles which have accumulated should be removed. Display the full value of your storage and utility spaces.

7. Step high - step low. Prospects will do just that unless all stairways are cleared of objects. Avoid cluttered appearances and possible injuries.

8. Closet illusions. Clothes properly hung, shoes, hats and other articles neatly placed will make closets appear adequate.

9. Dear to her heart is the kitchen. Colorful curtains in harmony with the floor and counter tops add appeal for the Lady of the House.

10. Check and double check bathrooms. Bright, clean bathrooms sell homes.

11. For the rest of your life. Bedrooms are always outstanding features. Arrange them neatly.

MEMBER OF THE NATIONAL ASSOCIATION OF REALTORS   REALTOR®

FIGURE 7–3 *(continued)*

SHOWING THE HOUSE

12. Can you see the light? Illumination is a welcome sign. For after-dark inspections turn on your lights, from the porch on through. The prospect will feel a glowing warmth otherwise impossible to attain.

13. "Three's a crowd." More will lose the sale. Avoid having too many people present during inspections. The prospect will feel like an intruder and will hurry through the house. It is better to be away from the home when it is being shown.

14. Music is mellow -- but not when showing a house. Shut off the radio - it distracts. Let the salesman and the buyer talk, free of disturbances.

15. Love me, love my dog does not apply in house selling. Keep pets out of the way - preferably out of the house.

16. Silence is golden. Be courteous but do not force conversation with the prospect. He is there to inspect your house -- not to pay a social call.

17. Be it ever so humble. Never apologize for the appearance of your home. After all, it has been lived in. Let our trained salesman answer any objections that are raised. This is his job.

18. In the shadows. Please do not tag along with the prospect and the salesman. He knows the buyer's requirements and can better emphasize the features of your house when alone. You will be called if needed.

19. Putting the cart before the horse. Trying to dispose of furniture and other furnishings to the prospect before he has purchased the house loses the sale.

20. A word to the wise. Do not discuss price, terms, possession or other features with the customers. Refer them to us. We are better equipped to bring the negotiation to a favorable conclusion with all due dispatch.

* * * * *

We ask that you show your home to prospective customers by appointment only through this office. Your cooperation will be appreciated and will lead to a more prompt consummation of the sale.

* * * * *

040/7/76

GEORGE REALTY CO./2768 south wadsworth boulevard · denver, colorado 80227 · 303/989-1870 questions about the technical aspects of the field, many salespeople are not competent.

"Certainly trust and honesty and sincerity and appearance are important. But it is *vitally* important for the individual to know what he is doing."

Dan Bloomquist explains that sellers list "with me because I live in the area and because over the last two or three years I have listed at least 42 percent of the homes for sale in the area. I know the area and exactly what has been sold, and I can meet the appraiser with the best comps. I know all the model names. Most other real estate salespersons don't know what model they are in. I know the square footage in each model. I know the room dimensions. I don't have to measure them any more. I think I impress the seller by being very knowledgeable."

Like Bloomquist, Don Nourse is so knowledgeable about his area that even lenders call him to verify current comparables. "I work very closely with the lenders, so they all know me, and I can handle their problems. I try to make the owners realize they are getting an advantage by working with me."

It would seem, in short, that the top listors have the most "know-how."

ONE- OR TWO-VISIT PRESENTATION?

There is a divergence of opinion among listors over whether to employ a one-visit or a two-visit approach.

Dave McGinnis says that although many salespeople seem to pick up listings on a single half-hour visit and then are on their way, he allots himself four hours and two trips.

On his first visit he introduces himself, explains his procedures, and collects data. "After introducing myself, I spend a few moments to make the people feel at ease instead of getting right into the listing process. I want to make them feel that they are working with a person rather than a broker. Once I have the feeling that they think of me as a reasonable, nice person, then I explain the listing process."

Following that, Dave goes through the house, getting all his measurements and observing its overall condition. "Before I leave, I tell them not to do anything until I get back to them—especially if it is an open listing. I stress that the price at which they now have the house on the open listing may be too low. I then go back to my office and prepare my analysis."

Sarah Catherine Holley explains that one of the reasons she always makes a two-visit listing approach is that she gets an idea of the sellers' personalities by studying the furnishings on her first visit. This helps her deal with the sellers on the second visit. Also, since many of the people whose homes she lists turn into buyers, making two visits gives her additional insights into the things they like and their tastes in general.

Charles Howe points out that the "general public thinks there is nothing to selling real estate. Most of them want to sell it themselves for a while." For this reason he thinks it important to take measurements and evaluate the overall condition of the property on the first visit. When he returns with his market analysis, he presents a wealth of accumulated information in a step-by-step fashion so that the sellers realize how unprepared they are to transact the sale themselves.

On the other hand, there are those like Loretta Baginski who make a one-visit presentation. But "I go in prepared. I find out everything I need to know beforehand. I've got my information, my comparables, my materials. I know I can handle the situation. I get the listing. In fact, I've never gone when someone has called me regarding listing and not gotten the listing."

What the listor *should* know about the prospect and the property before making his or her presentation sharpens the edge the listing pros have over others.

THE "LISTING PACKAGE"

Whether employing a one- or a two-visit listing interview, every top listor agrees that it is necessary to accumulate certain information before making the actual listing presentation.

The top listors are not satisfied with the minimal facts: name, address and telephone number, environmental amenities (trees, lawns, and so on), property conditions (needs painting, carpentry, and so on), and a check of MLS to note, say, that three comparable homes have sold within the last several months at a price spread of $9,500, that there has been an expiration on another, and that four are currently on the market.

Gathering information of this kind is only the beginning of the "prelisting homework" done by top listors.

"I don't believe there is any magic formula," comments Dave McGinnis. "It's really not too difficult because the people I'm working against are so unorganized and because they act like order takers.

They go in, and the seller *tells them* what kind of listing they are going to get and what kind of price they are going to list it for."

Following are the ingredients of a typical "listing package." Also noted are sources of information that have been described in earlier chapters. If the real estate salesperson does not have access to the various REDI volumes, he or she may obtain the same information by going to the county offices.

1. The prospect's name (telephone book, ownership roll, Alpha index).

2. The prospect's mailing address, if different than the property address (ownership roll).

3. The prospect's home telephone number (telephone book, Crisscross directories).

4. A legal description of the property (ownership roll).

5. The dimensions of the property and/or a plat map, if available (aerial, property identification map, county courthouse, *Appraiser's Handbook*).

6. The purchase price, the purchase date, and subsequent improvements to the property (deeds at county courthouse, title company —the *Appraiser's Handbook* will identify the deed book and the page number).

7. The assessed value of the property, plus taxes and exemptions (ownership roll, *Appraiser's Handbook*).

8. Details on any other properties owned by the prospect, particularly the types of property (Alpha index, ownership roll).

9. Neighborhood positives, such as schools, churches, and shopping (aerial, ownership roll, drive-by).

10. Neighborhood negatives, such as commercial encroachments (aerial, ownership roll, county courthouse, drive-by).

11. Area amenities, such as travel routes, recreation areas, and public safety (aerial, ownership roll).

12. Up-to-date information on mortgage-lending conditions (MLS books, Realty Sales Service, lenders).

13. A description of the improvements, such as the number of bedrooms and baths, age, the square footage of the buildings and the lot and the zoning requirements (*Appraiser's Handbook,* county assessor's office).

14. A complete "Comparative Market Analysis" (MLS books, Realty Sales Service, ownership roll, *Appraiser's Handbook*) (see Figure 7-4).

FIGURE 7–4
Sample Comparative Market Analysis Form

George
realty company
REALTOR

2768 south wadsworth boulevard · denver, colorado 80227 · 303 989-1870

C O M P A R A T I V E   M A R K E T   A N A L Y S I S

By: _____
Date: _____

Property Address: _____
Legal Description: _____

FOR SALE NOW	BDRMS	BATHS	FAM. RM. REC. RM.	GARAGE	BSMT	FIRE-PLACE	SQ. FT.	LIST PRICE	DAYS ON MKT

SOLD IN PAST 12 MONTHS	BDMRS	BATHS	FAM. RM. REC. RM.	GARAGE	BSMT	FIRE-PLACE	SQ. FT.	LIST PRICE	DAYS ON MKT	DATE SOLD	SALE PRICE	TERMS

SUBJECT PROPERTY									

AREA EVALUATION:

Assets _____ Drawbacks _____

Area Market Conditions _____ Recommended Terms _____

Top Competitive Market Value.........$ _____
Probable Final Sales Price.........$ _____
    TOTAL COSTS.........$ _____
    ESTIMATED NET PROCEEDS.........$ _____

FACTORS NECESSARY FOR A SUCCESSFUL SALE:

1. Is the home in top condition? (Landscaping, paint, carpets, draperies, etc.)
2. Is the price competitive with others on the market?
3. Are the terms attractive? (Good assumption? VA-FHA offered? Owner carry 2nd?)
4. Are homes in the area selling within reasonable time?

COMMENTS _____
_____
_____
_____

004/7/76

THE QUESTION OF PRICE

Charles Howe believes that the real estate salesperson wins the prospect's acceptance of the market analysis by showing what he or she did to develop the recommended value. "Even though you can arrive at the figure in your head because you are in the business seven days a week, you must still explain the process to the client."

Dave McGinnis explains that upon returning to the sellers after accumulating the information for his listing package, he goes through a step-by-step explanation of the market analysis and how it was done. By the time he is finished—it usually takes an hour—there is "no way they can dispute my figures because of the way I go over the analysis.

"And I'll never take a listing unless I've made a market analysis so that everyone is aware of what the proper price range should be. I never take a listing for less than 90 days. I never promise a whole lot of advertising. I never promise we will sell the property. I always make certain that my clients realize we will give our best efforts to marketing the property but that it is impossible to control the market.

"Even after I have invested all that time, if the sellers still insist on an open listing or on *overpricing* the property, I walk away from it. Because if you take it, you are giving in to them. And that's the worst thing you can do. I always tell them that this is my judgment and that I do not want to be responsible for mistakes that may result from an improperly handled listing."

All the top listors agree that it is necessary to be armed with all the facts. Unless the listor handles the preparation of the market analysis competently, he will not get the listing. Or if he does, he will have problems later.

Says Rick Niday, "When you have as many companies as we do here in Des Moines, you run into a bidding war. But I refuse to get involved. After I develop and explain my comps, I advise the prospect that I will not be a part of a bidding war. I will not add $5,000 to the value of a $40,000 house just to get the listing."

Sarah Catherine Holley also refuses to accept a listing if the people are not cooperative. "There is no point in having a listing that won't sell. I recommend that they list their home with another real estate broker."

Joyce Steffen adds, "It's dishonest—and a waste of time."

"A part of getting good listings," comments Everett Sanburn, "is pricing them so that they will sell. A lot of people have inflated ideas about what their property is worth. And those ideas are sometimes hard to overcome.

"I usually say jokingly, 'I'd like to sell your house at $100,000, but you and I both know that I can't do that, don't we? We will try to price the house to get you every penny that we can. But the other fellow has to put up the money, and ultimately he's the one who's going to say what your house is worth. We need to price the house so that we can get him to look at it. Because if he doesn't look, then he doesn't buy.' "

McGinnis stresses that even if someone were willing to pay an excessive price, when the time comes to finance the transaction, "the deal may fall through because the lender may not agree."

"The easiest way to get a listing is to put the highest price on the property," says Charles Howe. If Howe has any inkling that the owners are working with other brokers, he warns them against selecting the broker who will list their property at the highest price. He advises them to select the broker whom they are convinced knows most about the business.

Carole Kelby says that she brings her comps with her and deals with the sellers in a very positive manner. If she wants to list a house for $49,000 and the owners insist on listing it for $54,500, Carole tells them, "You asked me to come here, and you want the benefit of my knowledge and my experience. This is the price I want to take it at.

"Now, if it makes you feel better, we will try listing it for two weeks at your price, with the understanding—and it must be with this understanding—that if no people are coming through the house, we will drop the price every two weeks until we get to the price I suggest.

"But I do want to warn you that there is nothing worse than a shopworn listing. All the real estate agents out there are showing people homes. And by doing a good job for those people, the agents know that their clients will be a source of referrals.

"The agents don't want to show the buyers an overpriced house because then the buyers will think that the agents are trying to put something over on them. That's number one.

"And number two. If a house has been on the market four or five months and has not sold, every real estate agent has that human feeling, 'I wonder what's the matter with that house.' And it becomes a shopworn listing.

"Listen. You are talking $55,000. And I am talking $50,000. Let's hit a happy medium and try it for a couple of weeks at $52,900 and then start to bring the price down."

Rosamond Shaw believes that the missing element, either in the real estate salesperson's approach to clients or in the seller's approach to others, is common sense. "If you really sit down and think these problems out, the solution usually becomes very obvious. Try and put yourself in the other fellow's shoes. How would you feel then? And get the seller to think the same way.

"Like this fellow yesterday was screeching, 'The price should be higher!' I said, 'Fine. You are going down to Florida. You see two houses, and one costs $1,000 more than the other because the owner has to pay his own commission. What's your reaction?' He said, 'Well, it's not my problem!' I said, 'That's the answer.'

"I work on the old Chinese principle, 'Never let anybody lose face.' You can't tell the sellers they are foolish. You can't talk them out of it. But you can have them put themselves in the other fellow's shoes and make them see how he feels."

Along those same lines, Joyce Steffen remarks that sellers sometimes complain about her analysis by saying, "But the one up the street sold for _____ dollars, and mine is a better house."

In addition to drawing on her facts and pointing out the differences, Joyce replies, "Mr. and Mrs. _____, my opinion is irrelevant. And how do you know you can believe me? What I am giving you is objective information on value out in the marketplace.

"Everybody thinks his own house is the best. But the incoming buyer has no prejudices in your favor or in the other seller's favor. All he's going to ask is, 'How many bedrooms? How many baths? What's the condition?' and so forth."

A PREPARED BOOKLET OR AN "OFF-THE-CUFF" CONVERSATION?

Joyce's market analysis is contained in a booklet that she leaves with the sellers. The booklet also contains literature about her company, information on properties she has listed and sold, and an explanation of the services she and her associates will perform for the sellers to make their move as easy as possible.

Ruth Hubbard also presents all her facts in writing. "I don't care if they are considering ten brokers. I gather all my facts and personally write them up. And I leave this information with the owners."

When Dave McGinnis first started in the business, he made a number of visual aids to show sellers during his listing presentation.

Among them were charts and graphs showing what percentage of the market the sellers themselves could draw from as compared with the percentage of buyers a real estate broker would make available to them. Since then, Dave has committed these things to memory, and he no longer uses the book, though he continues to follow the steps.

In other words, although top listors agree that a market analysis is necessary, they are about evenly divided over whether or not to prepare a written presentation of the other elements discussed during the listing interview.

Carole Kelby allows approximately two hours for her presentation. "By the time I cover my market analysis, give the owners all the negatives and all the positives, tell them the worst that can happen to them and the best that can happen to them—by that time, there is no question about their listing with me."

Most of the top listors agree with Paul Manners that "the buyer usually knows what his costs will be, whereas the seller often does not." For this reason, a part of their presentation includes a computation of the seller's estimated net proceeds. As Ruth Hubbard notes, "People are really not interested in gross. They want to know what they are going to leave with at the closing table."

Most of the top listors also share Eileen Wallin's conviction that it is important to assure the prospect that a skillful listor "just won't let the listing sit there waiting for it to be sold. He will solicit other offices." Mike Knapp remarks, "I keep my ears open around the office to discover what the people in the office are looking for and push them toward my listing."

Gary Shapiro states emphatically, "Most real estate salespeople seem primarily concerned with the image and with institutional promotion directed toward buyers and sellers. That is important. But the *most* important people are internal industry people—those who end up selling one's listings over and over and over again.

"I've got a competitor like that. Because we have had successful dealings in the past and because I make it a point to keep in touch with him, he has become much more aware of my listings and ends up pushing them."

CUSTOMARY OBJECTIONS

Most of the top listors approach their prospects with a very positive attitude. These listors are confident of their knowledge and their skills.

This does not mean, however, that they do not encounter objections. The bulk of such objections arise with respect to the seller's need for a real estate broker, which we have discussed earlier. Here we will mention a few others.

Saving the commission is, of course, a common objection. Often, however, the seller will not express this concern. Yet it remains in his mind. For this reason, the real estate salesperson must be prepared to offer the seller ample justification for listing with a real estate broker.

In resolving this objection, Rosemary Kane may have an edge over mainland real estate salespeople. For Hawaii sellers, particularly "if they are leaving the island, it is advantageous to have a real estate broker. They may lose money by selling their property themselves since they are untrained and really don't know real estate values."

In answer to the complaint that real estate brokers charge a fee, Charles Howe replies, "If you can sell your own property, more power to you. But if you need someone to help you sell it, then that's what I'm spending six or seven days a week doing, and it's simply a service. And, Mr. Client, you have to look at it like that.

"If you could take care of your own teeth, you wouldn't have to go to a dentist. If you could handle your own legal difficulties, you wouldn't have to hire an attorney. And if you can't sell your own house, you will need a real estate broker. As far as the commission charge is concerned, you must look at it as a payment for service."

Lee Burch considers it indispensable to know the reason for selling. Only after that does she confront the seller's reluctance to pay a broker's commission. "The buyer isn't going to pay you a commission, Mr. Seller. Therefore, if you are asking $40,000 for your house, his calculator immediately starts going to deduct 7 percent.

"We can get you as much as you can get yourself. And in all probability, we can get enough additional to enable you to pay the commission."

And that is true, insists Mrs. Burch. "Most of the time owners sell their property for less than the fair market value."

Lee always asks prospects how they established their asking price. "They will often say something to this effect, 'Well, we heard the people across the street sold their house for _____ number of dollars. And we think our home is worth that." At that point, Lee explains her market analysis.

Eunice Reass mentions this objection, "We really believe you, but we are having difficulty in deciding *between your company and* _____ *company.*" To this, Eunice counters, "Well, if there were a better company, I would be with *that* company."

Eunice stresses the importance of one's company. "I don't believe there is anything more valuable to an agent than a reputable firm. It doesn't have to be big. It just has to be reputable."

To "I'm going to *list with my friend* _____," Maurice Johnson answers, "Well, that is fine. Does he sell real estate full time?" If the reply is negative, Maurey points out, "Well now, Mr. Prospect, you realize that this is going to be one of the largest transactions you are going to make in your lifetime. You really should be giving it to a broker who knows the area and to an individual who sells real estate fulltime. And I am a full-time real estate broker."

If the prospect tells Johnson that his friend does sell real estate full time, Maurey may then ask for the name of the friend's firm. "Well, _____ is a good company. I'm not denying that fact. But _____ does not sell many homes in this area. Therefore, it is unlikely to have buyers for this area. We do. And we have that advantage over _____. Do you remember the house at _____ that was listed for three months. It was listed with an out-of-the-area broker. Within the last month we listed and sold that same house."

Similarly, Joyce Steffen tells prospective sellers that "buyers will look for the company which has the most listings in an area, employs full-time salespeople, and provides the best service. And since it doesn't cost them anything to look, they will come to us. If the buyers come to us, wouldn't it be wise for the seller to come to us?"

When told by a prospect that he intends to list with a specific real estate salesperson, Everett Sanburn quite boldly asks the prospect what he knows about the salesperson's position and performance record. Invariably the prospect makes some general remark to the effect that the person "just sells."

To this, Everett declares, "Well, that's fine. I'm not trying to take anything from _____. You may not know his record, but this is my record. I've sold 96 percent of my listings. I've sold more houses than anyone else in Pounder and Company, a long-respected firm. Would you rather deal with me or an unknown?"

Sanburn recognizes that this may sound a bit strong. "But if you don't tell them, they're not going to know it. It took a lot of hard work for me to get to my position. And a person doesn't achieve anything by sitting on his duff!"

OPEN LISTINGS VERSUS EXCLUSIVE LISTINGS

In some areas of the country, brokers are willing to settle for open listings. Dave McGinnis is in one such area. A couple of years ago he analyzed a year's listing activity. He discovered that 90 percent of his *exclusive listings* sold but that only one of 58 *open listings* sold.

"It was evident," notes Dave, "that my least productive time had been spent in handling open listings. Although I had a good year, it would have been much better if I had put my efforts into more profitable listing activity. I discovered that I had been making listings just for the sake of having listings, regardless of whether or not they were good listings.

"Now I will never take an open listing. If a person will take his time and work harder to get fewer but better listings, the listings will sell quicker, and the benefits will snowball farther."

In his approach to open listings, Dave suggests to sellers, first, that with an open listing, having to pay a dual commission is a possibility —the owner may have to pay twice for the sale.

Second, he notes that real estate agencies usually do not make an all-out effort on their open listings. They concentrate on their exclusive listings because they are guaranteed their commission on those. Third, sellers who use an exclusive have only one broker to deal with, whereas sellers who use an open listing have to go through the listing process with several brokers.

What startles McGinnis most is that few listors even bother to approach the seller with the idea of the exclusive. He claims that defining the advantages of the exclusive enables him to obtain this better type of listing rather easily. And "the better the quality of the listing, the better *everyone* is going to be."

8

Open House

PURPOSES OF THE OPEN HOUSE

The *open house* functions to:

1. Accommodate sellers.
2. Obtain buyers.
3. Produce further listings.

"Indeed I hold open house," says Loretta Baginski. "I haven't sold a lot of the houses I've held open. But I do it because I think it's important. You've got to make your sellers feel that you're earning what they're paying you."

Mrs. Burch prefers not to hold open house, since knocking on doors or contacting FBSOs is more profitable for her. "I know it's very profitable for other real estate salespeople. But not for me. However, when I list a property, I always ask, 'How do you feel about having open house?' Of course, if the owners say, 'We'd like to have it held open,' and if I think it is a house that would get traffic, I'll go along with it."

Eunice Reass agrees. "I very rarely sold the house I was holding open, but I usually sold something else. But my willingness to hold open house always reassured the homeowners that I was interested in them."

Jim Kunkel is enthusiastic about holding open house, "mainly because I like to meet people face-to-face." And also because holding open house generates listings and sales for him.

"If I have a dozen couples through, I'll sell at least two right away. To me, that is productive time spent." Jim may not do anything with the remaining ten for months, but on the other hand, "I've held open house, gotten four prospects through, and sold all four within a month.

"I can put a chain together as a result of one open house. One Saturday when I had an hour to spare I called the owner and went out and threw an 'Open House' sign in front of his home. Only one couple came in. But in a matter of 60 days that one couple led me to $6,000 worth of income.

"The couple walked in but didn't like the house I was showing. However, as a result of our conversation I listed their house, sold them another home, and got three other listings by holding their home open. It all just snowballs."

Jim keeps a couple of directional signs and an "Open House" sign in his car. If he has some spare time, he will head for a property he can hold open. "All I care about is getting somebody to talk to. From there, I can go in just any direction."

HOW TO USE OPEN HOUSE TO
OBTAIN ADDITIONAL LISTINGS

Most salespeople hold open house in order to service the listing and generate buyers.

However, the open house is also one of the most effective devices for obtaining additional listings, a fact about which many salespeople are not aware.

Like all the other methods the top listors employ, using the open house as a source of listings requires effort. But the method is quite simple.

On the Thursday preceding a Sunday open house, the listor will prepare a brief letter or postcard announcing the date, time, and place of the open house. This announcement is hand-addressed to the occupants of the houses surrounding the home to be shown.

The announcements are posted on Thursday so that the addressees will receive them before the Sunday showing, but not so far in advance that they will forget the event.

If the open house is scheduled, say, for 2:00 to 5:00 P.M., beginning at about 11:00 A.M., the listor will knock on the door of each home to which the announcement was mailed.

The listor will be brief. "Good morning. I am Zip Zap of Professional Realty. I mailed you a letter announcing the open house I am having this afternoon at 1024 Juniper. Did you receive it?"

The answer will generally be "Yes" or "No." Sometimes the answer will be "Yes—we intend to come" or "No—we are not interested."

Regardless of the answer, the listor says, "The owners will not be home during the open house, but they want you to know that you and any of your friends are welcome to inspect the house. Thank you."

If at all possible, the listor avoids any conversation. If the occupant promises to come, *you have a prospect!* But do not engage in any conversation. Merely say, "Good. See you later." Leave and go to the next door.

At houses where no one answers your knock, leave a note that says what you would have told the occupants:

> Sorry I missed you. I merely stopped to remind you of the open house I am having at 1024 Juniper from 2:00 to 5:00 this afternoon.
>
> Although Mr. and Mrs. Seller will not be home during the showing, they want you to know that you are most welcome.

Slip this note in the handle of the front door or some other conspicuous place so that the occupants will see it when they return.

If you have a *good* photocopying machine, you will find it just as effective and certainly less time consuming to write one note and reproduce it. You should probably run off copies for about one third the number of houses you intend to approach. Usually that many occupants will not be home.

If you reproduce a note written with a black felt-tip pen, it will appear to have been individually written. If your office is not equipped to reproduce the note, you can have this done inexpensively at a nearby commercial outlet.

The number of announcements you mail will depend on the number of houses surrounding the listed property that you wish and have the time to contact Sunday morning.

If there are eight homes on each side of the street, then you might contact the seven on the same side of the street as the "house for sale" and the eight across the street. That makes 15.

You might also contact the homes on the two adjacent blocks. That amounts to another 32 homes. Those 47 houses are about all you will have the time to visit. It takes about an hour and a half to canvass 50 houses.

Should the property not sell immediately, the next time you hold the house open, you might contact the occupants of houses in the remaining directions. Thus, if you canvassed the blocks to the east and west of the listing the first time, the next time you might canvass the blocks north and south of the property. Thereafter, you can continue to fan out in alternating directions.

It is rare not to have at least one occupant show up. And usually there are more. Those who come are (1) snoopers, (2) prospective buyers, or (3) potential listings.

It is highly unlikely that snoopers will come, although this has happened. In general, people seem to feel that snooping in a neighbor's home is a gross invasion of privacy; whereas snooping in a stranger's is not.

Regardless of their reasons, the neighbors who show up mean business. They may be searching for a nearby house for a friend or relative. They may be renters who wish to buy. They may be homeowners who wish to exchange their house for one that they consider better. Or they may be homeowners who are getting ready to sell and are trying to establish a market value by comparing properties.

The system described above is one of the most effective for uncovering a listing prospect before any other real estate salesperson knows what is taking place. It is even a way for a perceptive listor to uncover a homeowner's subliminal intentions.

But it must be emphasized that when one of the neighbors appears, the listor should "switch on and operate at full bore."

HOW TO CONDUCT THE OPEN HOUSE

You will recognize the neighbors who were at home when you called, but you must ask all other visitors how they learned about the open house.

If you use a guest register, as does Colleen Rosinbum, you may add a column in the book for the answer.

"I don't let any people come through the house without signing their name, address, and phone number," explains Colleen. Few object.

Colleen feels that the guest register is absolutely essential, especially if she is swamped and cannot qualify people individually. The next day or the day after, she phones the prospects and tries to arrange an appointment with them for the purpose of showing them other properties or listing their homes.

"When people enter, I always say, 'Please sign the guest register, and then I'll take you on a tour of the home.' " While showing the home to visitors, Colleen tries to find out why they are looking at that particular house, where they live, whether or not they are renting, and whether or not they intend to sell their present home.

"Often I will set up an appointment at that time to look at their property and evaluate its marketability. I explain that this will put them in a better position to know in what price range they should be looking. I also suggest that they put their home on the market and make its sale subject to finding another home of their choice. All of this really works very well."

Jim Kunkel also probes for information. "Be sincere and honest. But don't beat around the bush. Get straight to the point. 'Why are you making a change? Why do you want to sell your house now? Do you really think you should?' Being frank and honest gains me more business. In the long run it pays off. Just be square with people."

To those who feel squeamish about asking what may seem to be rather prying questions, Jim replies, "It's your business to get this information so you can make a decent judgment. Otherwise, how do you know whether you can help them?"

After introducing himself to visitors, says Don Nourse, "The first thing I ask them, so that I don't get trapped, is, 'Are you from this area? Are you familiar with Turtle Rock?' I want to know what they are doing at my open house. If they come from Santa Monica, I ask, what brings you down here?' "

Don begins to qualify people as soon as they enter the house. Soon he has them engaged in a conversation to develop rapport.

Whether Don shows the visitors around or lets them look on their own depends "on how we come across with each other when we meet. But I don't usually try to sell the house I'm holding open. Don't become a used car salesman.

"Let the people look at the house. Point out the good parts, but don't try to sell the house to them. You'd be surprised how many people wonder why the hell you're not trying to sell it to them.

"And react. I've discovered a lot of times that people are checking you out to determine whether they should let you list their house."

Don holds open house in his farm every weekend, usually from noon until 4:30 on either Saturday or Sunday and sometimes on both days. He does as well on Saturday as on Sunday.

Don gives visitors to his open house "a little package of the area." This includes a map of the community and diagrams of the various floor plans available within the homes of his farm. The packet reinforces his standing as the listing authority within his community.

Whatever the reasons for holding an open house, all listors agree that the sellers should not be at home while it is being held.

QUESTIONS THAT THE LISTOR SHOULD BE PREPARED TO ANSWER

For a summary of the types of questions most real estate salespersons believe that the listor should be prepared to answer at an open house, see Figure 8–1.

FIGURE 8–1
Typical Questions a Listor Should Be Prepared to Answer at an Open House

1. Where do children attend school?
   a. All ages.
   b. Know the location.
   c. Know the distance.
2. Where are the parochial schools?
   a. What do they cost?
3. Where are the private schools?
   a. What do they cost?
   b. What grades do they handle?
4. Where can people play golf?
   a. How much summer golf?—how much winter golf?
   b. Must a cart be rented?
5. Where may people play tennis?
   a. Public or private?
   b. What does it cost?
   c. Courts lighted?

FIGURE 8–1 (*continued*)

6. Where may people ski?
   a. Distance?
   b. Rates?
   c. Accommodations?

7. Where may one go boating?
   a. How far?
   b. How much?
   c. Public or private?
   d. Types?

8. Where may one swim?
   a. What does it cost?

9. Where can children get swimming lessons?
   a. What does it cost?

10. Is there a nearby beach?
    a. Miles?
    b. Time?

11. How far is it to shopping?
    a. Convenience store.
    b. Groceries.
    c. Shopping malls.

12. How far is it to an interstate highway or a turnpike?

13. Is there a community association?
    a. What does it cost?
    b. Whom does one see to join?

14. Is there a community recreation center?
    a. What does membership cost?

15. What other entertainment and recreational facilities are available?
    a. Types?
    b. Names?
    c. Locations?

16. What cultural opportunities exist? (Theaters, libraries, museums, symphony orchestras, and so on.)
    a. Types?
    b. Names?
    c. Locations?

17. Where are the nearest hospitals?
    a. Names?
    b. Locations?

18. Who built the houses?

FIGURE 8–1 *(concluded)*

19. What kinds of people live in the neighborhood?
    a. Occupations?
    b. Where do the people in the neighborhood come from?
20. When were the houses built?
21. Does the area have sewers?
    a. When can they be expected?
22. Where are the churches?
    a. What denominations?
23. What has the neighborhood growth pattern been?
24. What has been sold in the area?
    a. How much?
    b. When? (See Comparative Market Analysis Form, p. 119.)
25. What is for sale now?
    a. How much?
    b. How long? (See Comparative Market Analysis Form, p. 119.)

9

A Final Word

It is hoped that this book, which you opened with expectation, will close with profit.

The book has not been intended to tell you how to perform the rudimentary steps of establishing your annual goals, completing the listing agreement, or preparing a listing brochure. There are basic texts that will introduce you to the instruments of the trade.

But just as the tools of the apprentice help produce feats of craftsmanship in the hands of the master carpenter, so the sources available to all real estate salespersons become wands of success in the hands of the top producers.

Every real estate salesperson should be able to learn something from years of laborious experience. It is the smart real estate salesperson, however, who can learn from a book. And in this book you have the opportunity to profit from the advice of people in the elite top 5 percent of residential real estate earnings, achievers whose income from listings alone is the envy of many.

PERSONAL QUALITIES OF THE SUCCESSFUL LISTOR

These top listors stress the importance of knowing what information the real estate salesperson should have about prospects and property, knowing where to obtain that information, and knowing how to package and present it. But they also suggest that other factors are involved in becoming a skilled listor. Let's consider what they have to say.

They all agree that to attract the attention of the seller favorably the real estate salesperson must present a nice *appearance.* Before you even speak, the prospect looks at you. This is his first impression, and it is lasting.

You must look successful. Your clothing must be good but not gaudy.

You should drive a nice, clean automobile. It should be new, or only a few years old, but it should not be ostentatious. It should be of a make and model that most nearly identifies you with your customary clientele.

Also included in your prospect's impression of you are your mannerisms, bearing, and speech. All of these factors add up to form a picture which the prospect compares with his image of how a successful, professional real estate salesperson should look, speak, and act.

"An attractive package in a supermarket will be more appealing and more outstanding to a customer than an unattractive package," explains Mike Silverman. "And that goes for human beings."

Closely associated with a nice appearance are a positive attitude and a good personality.

Having a positive *attitude* can mean having confidence in yourself, having self-esteem, and having a reasonable assurance that you are capable of providing the service you are offering. It is often thought of as the "power of positive thinking" concept popularized by Norman Vincent Peale. Napoleon Hill has formulated it in the axiom "Whatever the mind of man can conceive, and believe, he can achieve."

That optimism is also evidenced in a statement by Loretta Baginski: "When someone calls and asks me to come and talk about a listing, as far as I am concerned I have the listing."

The top producers also think of positive attitude in terms similar to those expressed by Ray Novotny, who says, "What it all boils down to is being a sociable person and putting other people's interests above your own. If you have a bad day at home, you need to put aside any disagreeable feelings when working with clients.

"It's an attitude business, and if sellers see that you are having an uptight day they will not be comfortable with you. Also, they will wonder, "How many times does he have an uptight day?' or 'If I feel this way, what are buyers going to feel?'

"You meet people through people, and you must be able to get along even with people whose personalities are the polar opposite of what you prefer."

They all agree that to attract the attention of the seller favorably the real estate salesperson must present a nice *appearance*. Before you even speak, the prospect looks at you. This is his first impression, and it is lasting.

You must look successful. Your clothing must be good but not gaudy.

You should drive a nice, clean automobile. It should be new, or only a few years old, but it should not be ostentatious. It should be of a make and model that most nearly identifies you with your customary clientele.

Also included in your prospect's impression of you are your mannerisms, bearing, and speech. All of these factors add up to form a picture which the prospect compares with his image of how a successful, professional real estate salesperson should look, speak, and act.

"An attractive package in a supermarket will be more appealing and more outstanding to a customer than an unattractive package," explains Mike Silverman. "And that goes for human beings."

Closely associated with a nice appearance are a positive attitude and a good personality.

Having a positive *attitude* can mean having confidence in yourself, having self-esteem, and having a reasonable assurance that you are capable of providing the service you are offering. It is often thought of as the "power of positive thinking" concept popularized by Norman Vincent Peale. Napoleon Hill has formulated it in the axiom "Whatever the mind of man can conceive, and believe, he can achieve."

That optimism is also evidenced in a statement by Loretta Baginski: "When someone calls and asks me to come and talk about a listing, as far as I am concerned I have the listing."

The top producers also think of positive attitude in terms similar to those expressed by Ray Novotny, who says, "What it all boils down to is being a sociable person and putting other people's interests above your own. If you have a bad day at home, you need to put aside any disagreeable feelings when working with clients.

"It's an attitude business, and if sellers see that you are having an uptight day they will not be comfortable with you. Also, they will wonder, "How many times does he have an uptight day?' or 'If I feel this way, what are buyers going to feel?'

"You meet people through people, and you must be able to get along even with people whose personalities are the polar opposite of what you prefer."

Tom Lawrence (of Lawrence, Leiter and Company, Midwest management consultants) also cautioned his listeners that all people should be treated as "introverts" until you got to know them. Following this practice, you could never go wrong, never offend anyone. Lawrence explained that this was because people gear their remarks so as not to hurt the introvert. And whatever they say, they cannot offend the extravert.

"For instance," Carole comments, "if you say to an introvert, 'Did you watch the football game this weekend?' and he replies, 'No, I was at the opera,' you are in trouble. But if you say to an extravert, 'Did you go to the opera?' he's likely to answer, 'No, I don't look at that stuff. But I did see a hell of a good football game!' In other words, the extravert will let everything bounce off, but you can alienate an introvert by making the wrong remark to him."

The third sales step is to establish *conviction* and *desire* in the prospect's mind. The listor achieves this by evincing a number of characteristics in combination. These include absolute honesty, moderate aggressiveness, successful performance, and again, knowledge. Sellers must have confidence that the listor is competent to represent them, "will not get them into trouble," and will render them a service.

Whether expressed in Everett Sanburn's terms, "People don't like to do business with a loser," or in Gary Shapiro's "Success breeds success," the point is that the seller is entrusting one of his most valuable possessions (perhaps his *most* valuable possession) to the listor.

As G. S. (Skip) Parker of Paul Semonin Company, Louisville, Kentucky, says, "You must convey to people that you can handle their property, that you know what you are doing, that you are not just getting a listing. If people get the idea that you are just out to get a listing, they won't list with you.

"Here in Louisville, sellers can list with 3,000 agents. But they don't want to just list their property. They want a competent service performed. They are not giving you a listing just to do you a favor. There are a lot of people they can do favors for.

"You must convey to people that you can do your job. That you know what you are doing."

As noted in an earlier chapter, persistence is essential. Also important are organization and a continual effort at self-improvement. Set goals, work out a plan, and follow that plan. Perform your tasks according to the "IOOI rule": *In Order Of Importance*. "This is not a

Tuesday afternoon business," says Loretta Baginski. "You need to be unselfish. And read, read everything you can get your hands on."

THE KEY TO A SUCCESSFUL CAREER

When the contributors you have met in this book were interviewed, after explaining what they had done to become top listors, almost without exception they remarked that they hoped their comments would be helpful to others, that they had tried to tell everything they knew about getting listings.

After all the interviews were completed, the fact that suddenly surged to the surface was that the methods these people use to obtain listings are available to all, but that what makes the methods effective are the persons who utilize them. These persons would be achievers in almost any occupation they pursued.

This common denominator—this key to a successful career and a successful life—is noted because it relates to a facet of psychology known as psycho-cybernetics.

"The most important psychologic discovery of this century is the discovery of the *self-image*," explains Maxwell Maltz, M.D., F.I.C.S., author of *Psycho-Cybernetics*. (p. 2)[1]

"The *self-image* is the key to human personality and human behavior. Change the self-image and you change the personality and the behavior. . . . The *self-image* sets the boundaries of individual accomplishment. It defines what you can and cannot do. Expand the self-image and you expand the areas of the possible. (p. ix)

"All your actions, feelings, behavior—even your abilities—are always consistent with this self-image. In short, you will act like the sort of person you conceive yourself to be." (p. 2)

As Dr. Maltz explains, man was created to achieve and to be successful. He is not a machine, but he has in him a built-in guidance system which, after being given a clearly defined goal, automatically "helps him get answers to problems, invent, write poetry, run a business, sell merchandise, explore new horizons in science, attain more peace of mind, develop a better personality, or achieve success in any other activity which is ultimately tied in to his living or makes for a fuller life." (p. 15)

---

1 *Psycho-Cybernetics*, Prentice-Hall, Inc., Englewood Cliffs, N.J., 1960, pages as shown.

The operations resemble those of a computer system. Once programmed by the intellect with a specific objective, man's servomechanism, if allowed to function, automatically attains its goal. Although the servomechanisms has been used by men like Edison, Ford, Emerson, Napoleon, Henry Kaiser, Conrad Hilton, and countless others, it has been mainly since the development of the analog computer and the digital computer that the science of cybernetics has recognized that man's brain and nervous system can achieve incredible results.

Whether or not successful, the listors interviewed are aware of the principles of psycho-cybernetics, it is plainly evident that they possess the *self-image* which is the essential ingredient for accomplishing a desired goal.

THE FUTURE OF THE REAL ESTATE PROFESSIONAL

A recent estimate discloses that the value of taxable U.S. real estate amounts to $2.6 trillion.

This amount becomes even more impressive if you compare it to the $970 billion combined value of stocks traded over the counter and on the New York and American stock exchanges, or to the $1.1 trillion in circulation and in savings accounts, or to the current gross national product of $1.2 trillion (see Figure 9–1).

Greater opportunities are yet to come in the field of real estate because of the growth of and shifting within our mobile society.

FIGURE 9–1
The Importance of Real Estate

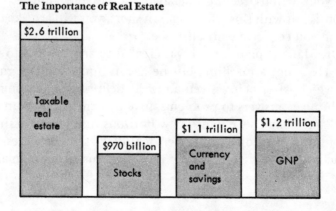

There are both ample and credible indicators and projections to convince any real estate professional that he or she is in the right place at the right time—now and into the foreseeable future.

According to reliable economic forecasters, even with a shifting mobile society, there will be population growth in every region of the country, as well as increased incomes.

Following the advice from the pros shared with you in this book, the listing goals you set *can* be realized. It is all within your control.

One final comment. Among the numerous sources of obtaining listings, one more must be indicated to complete the picture: a buyer today becomes a seller tomorrow. How the pros find and cultivate him is material for another book.

Index